Whole Earth Cooking
for the 80's

Whole Earth Cooking for the 80's

Healthy Food in Hard Times

By Sharon Cadwallader

St. Martin's Press
New York

Library of Congress Cataloging in Publication Data

Cadwallader, Sharon.
   Whole earth cooking for the 80's.

   1. Cookery. I. Title.
TX715.C126   641.5   80-27974
ISBN 0-312-87051-5

Design by: Falcaro & Tiegreen Ltd.
Illustrations by: Mary K. Tiegreen
10 9 8 7 6 5 4 3 2 1
First Edition

This book is dedicated
to a
healthier, whole earth
and
easier, hard times.

CONTENTS

❧INTRODUCTION❧

Since the publication nine years ago of my *Whole Earth Cookbook*, dietary awareness has increased significantly not only in the United States, but in the entire world. Our greater understanding of the relation of food quality to health has motivated us to change our eating habits, but so too are we aware that in many parts of the globe, food shortages are reaching crisis proportions.

This book is dedicated to the times. It can't be disputed that we are facing lean years ahead, and as we have to tighten our money belts, we may also have to cinch our waistbands. But although the transition to more judicious and economical eating may be difficult, especially for the many of us used to enjoying abundant food production, I feel the road is paved by the encouraging changes in our habits over the past decade. This book will, I hope, make future changes easier, more palatable.

The equation for the 80's balances how much food value we can obtain against our money and time spent. Food value in this case refers primarily to *protein value:* when we try to cut back on costs and length of preparation time for our meals, we inevitably tend to sacrifice the protein content of our foods. With this in mind, all the recipes in this book are designed to be economical, healthful, and reasonably quick to prepare. Since certain protein foods are more metabolically usable than others, I have tried to emphasize these foods in the recipes of this book. So these recipes defer to protein, but they are also selected and designed to offer as many of the *general* nutrients we need in relation to cost and preparation time. And as a planning and shopping guide, each recipe figures for the approximate cost, protein grams, and preparation time. (The protein and cost figures do not include the value of the accompaniments suggested at the beginning of each recipe.)

The recipes are designed to feed four or six people, depending on appetites, but most of them can be doubled or extended with very little effort. And for the smaller households they can be halved, or frozen for later use.

The cost of each recipe is necessarily approximate since food prices vary according to the seasons and geographical regions, and since the market prices at this writing will differ from those at the time you are using this. In most cases they will be higher and it will be necessary to add a percentage increase. However, the estimated costs here are based on regular supermarket prices without observing fluctuating production, market specials, or the economics of home gardening, freezing, and canning. Too, food prices are often whimsical and you may actually find some food costs have gone down.(Don't count on it, though.)

1

INTRODUCTION

The figures for protein grams for the recipes are based on information from the United States Department of Agriculture. They represent the total grams of protein for each dish and should be divided by the number of servings to get individual numbers. These figures, too, must be considered approximate since the age, quality, and specific preparation of food affects nutritional value, and, of course, we all digest and metabolize our food at a different rate. According to the National Research Council of the National Academy of Sciences the recommended daily protein requirement is 0.42 grams for each pound of body weight. Therefore, to figure out your individual protein need, just divide your body weight by two and the result is the approximate number of protein grams you require each day.

Because we are all pressed for time in today's busy world, the recipes have also been selected for their expedience in preparation in relation to cost and nutritional value. The preparation time estimated for each recipe includes the physical preparation and cooking time: marinating, chilling, and freezing time are not included.

I have not counted calories in this book because I am not addressing any special diet. However, recipe portions tend to be conservative—not only because of cost but because many of us are concerned about over-eating. I have tried to be spare with salt and fat, and I've included a substantial vegetarian section because of the increasing interest in vegetarian cooking.

Most of the suggested accompaniments to the recipes are recommended to nutritionally balance out the meal plan. But in the vegetarian section these suggestions are more important as they are designed to complete the protein balance of each recipe.

I should add that all these recipes can be considered just as ideas for creative cooks. Feel free to substitute and alter ingredients to your instincts, taste, and training. After all, America is a country of great cooks.

Sharon Cadwallader

VEGETARIAN DISHES

As of this writing, there are some 20 million vegetarians in the United States. Many exclusively vegetarian cookbooks are available, and restaurants specializing in vegetarian dishes have cropped up all over the continent. Certainly this is an understandable and welcome phenomenon since meat, and to some extent poultry and fish, as lone protein sources have been heavily criticized in the last few years. Their fat and cholesterol contents have been shown to affect health negatively, and it's now clear animals have been subject to questionable chemicals in their growth and diet which may be passed on up the food chain. Too, in farming, vegetarian protein offers more usable protein per acre when compared to animal grazing land. This is important to any country with a rapidly multiplying population and greater longevity.

VEGETARIAN DISHES

Vegetarian food sources—eggs, cheese, grains, legumes, nuts, seeds, and vegetables—can be combined easily to create delicious dishes that are generally economical. Eggs, grains, and legumes are especially reasonable and versatile sources of protein. Cheese and nuts (with the exception of peanuts, and, often, unroasted nuts) are expensive and should be purchased in bulk on special whenever it is possible. However, only small amounts are needed to add significant protein and flavor to a vegetarian dish. Seeds, too, are high in protein per ounce. When using any fresh vegetables it's always more economical to buy them in season.

Vegetarians have various affinities. Some eat a little fish and poultry, while others may eat fish but not poultry. Some eat neither, but they will eat eggs or cheese. Whatever one's personal preference, it is important to obtain complete protein for a proper diet. Briefly, nitrogen-containing amino acids are the essential components of protein. These amino acids (there are 22 in all) are vital to the formation and tone of body tissue. Many of them are manufactured in the body cells from nitrogen released from other protein, combined with fat and sugar, but eight amino acids cannot be produced by this process. These are referred to as the essential amino acids and are obtained traditionally from animal and dairy products. However, all amino acids are essential to good health. If one wishes to forego the eating of animal and dairy products that are rich in the eight essential amino acids, care must be given to obtaining and combining these amino acids from alternative sources in order to create a protein balance. I have selected and designed these vegetarian dishes with these in mind.

This section offers a variety of vegetable protein dishes. At the beginning of each recipe are suggested accompaniments that help you obtain balanced protein. These are often called ,rotein complements. You should keep these complements in mind as you plan vegetarian meals, but you should also feel free to experiment with seasonings and ingredients. Vegetarian cooking allows great license for creativity.

4

EGGPLANT & SPAGHETTI SAUCE

Approximate cost (including pasta): $4.50
Protein grams (including pasta): 100
Preparation time: 2 hours

If the kids don't see the eggplant, you may be able to fool them with this one. Serve with a tossed green salad.

6 tablespoons oil	¼ teaspoon fennel seed
1 medium onion, coarsely chopped	2 tablespoons fresh, minced parsley
1 small to medium eggplant, diced	½ teaspoon cinnamon
1 can (1-pound) tomatoes	2 teaspoons brown sugar
1 can (6-ounce) tomato paste	½ cup red wine
2½ cups water	1 cup sliced fresh mushrooms (optional)
1 can (2¼-ounce) sliced olives	¾ pound uncooked soy and whole-wheat (or whole-wheat) spaghetti
2 cloves garlic, mashed	Parmesan cheese, grated
1 teaspoon salt	
½ teaspoon dried oregano	
½ teaspoon dried basil	

Heat 3 tablespoons oil in a heavy pot or Dutch oven, and sauté onion until softened. Remove onion with slotted spoon. Add remaining oil and eggplant. Stir frequently because eggplant absorbs oil as it cooks. After 6 to 8 minutes, return onions to pot and add tomatoes, tomato paste, and water. Reduce heat to simmer. Add all other ingredients except wine, mushrooms, pasta, and cheese. Cover and simmer for 1½ to 2 hours. (The sauce will pick up flavor as it simmers.) Check occasionally and add water if necessary. Add wine and mushrooms during last 15 minutes. Cook pasta in boiling, salted water with a teaspoon or so of oil. Drain, rinse, and serve with sauce sprinkled with grated cheese. Serves 5 to 6.

�651Hint: The addition of salt and a little oil in cooking water for pasta prevents sticking.❥

LENTIL & EGGPLANT STEW

Approximate cost: $1.65
Protein grams: 150
Preparation time: 2 hours
Serve with coleslaw and Corn Muffins (page 88).

2	cups lentils	1	teaspoon dried oregano
2	quarts water		
1	medium onion, chopped	1	teaspoon dried basil
¼	cup olive oil	3	cloves garlic, mashed
1	medium eggplant, diced	¼	cup red wine vinegar
1	can (6-ounce) tomato paste		Salt and pepper
2	cups celery, chopped		Dash hot pepper sauce

Rinse lentils in cold water. In a soup pot, bring the 2 quarts water to boil and add lentils. Reduce heat, cover, and simmer for 1 hour. Sauté onion in medium frying pan in 2 tablespoons olive oil until softened. Transfer to soup pot. Add remaining oil to frying pan, and add eggplant. Sauté for 5 to 6 minutes, and then add to pot, along with tomato paste, celery, oregano, basil, garlic, and vinegar. Cover and simmer for another hour or so. Add water if necessary. Salt and pepper to taste. Add a dash of hot pepper sauce before serving. Serves 4 to 6.

SPINACH & CHEESE-STUFFED EGGPLANT CRÊPES

Approximate cost: $3
Protein grams: 120
Preparation time: 1 hour

These crêpes are somewhat time-consuming to prepare, but they are well worth the effort. Serve them with Soy and Wheat-Sesame Muffins (page 89) and a tossed green salad.

EGGPLANT:

1	1½- to 2-pound eggplant	1	egg
½	cup unbleached flour	1	cup milk
			Oil for frying
			Flour

STUFFING:

1 **package (10-ounce) frozen, chopped spinach**	2 **cups grated mozzarella cheese**
	1 **egg, lightly beaten**
	Salt

SAUCE:

1 **can (15-ounce) tomato sauce**	1½ **teaspoons dried basil**
½ **cup fresh, minced parsley**	

To prepare eggplant: Peel eggplant and slice lengthwise into 10-12 slices. Beat flour with egg and milk until smooth. Pour batter into shallow pan. Spread a thin layer of flour on a plate or other surface. Heat 2 tablespoons oil in large frying pan. Dip eggplant slices in flour, then coat with batter. Using remaining oil, fry over medium heat until browned on both sides and flexible enough to bend easily. Repeat this process until all slices of eggplant are prepared.

To prepare stuffing: Cook spinach according to package directions. Squeeze out excess water in tea towel. Mix spinach with cheese and egg. Salt lightly.

To prepare sauce: Mix tomato sauce with parsley and basil, and heat gently for 10 minutes.

To assemble crêpes: Put a small amount of stuffing on one end of an eggplant slice and roll up like a crêpe. Place rolls together in shallow baking pan. Pour sauce over rolls. Cover with foil or a lid, and bake in a 375-degree oven for 15 minutes or until hot and bubbly. Serves 4 to 6.

❺Hint: The best cheese wrapper for the refrigerator is aluminum foil, because it seals in the odor and prevents the cheese from drying.❾

BROWN-RICE CHEESEBURGERS

Approximate cost (not including bun): $2
Protein grams (not including bun): 95
Preparation time: 30 minutes

This is a good family supper, and because the burgers make good cold fare, the kids can take them to school as lunch sandwiches. Serve them with the garnishes listed for Whole-Wheat Hamburger Buns (page 86), accompanied by coleslaw or a tossed green salad.

3	tablespoons oil	2	large eggs, beaten
1	large onion, finely chopped	½	cup whole-wheat flour
1	cup finely chopped celery		Salt and pepper
½	cup fresh minced parsley		Oil for frying
3	cloves garlic, grated	1½	cups grated cheddar cheese
4	cups cooked Brown Rice (page 102)	½	cup mayonnaise
2	cups grated carrots	1	tablespoon soy sauce
		10	hamburger buns
			Sliced tomatoes

Heat oil in large frying pan, and sauté onion, celery, parsley, and garlic until well softened. Pour into large mixing bowl with rice, carrots, eggs, and flour. Salt and pepper to taste. Form into large hamburger-shaped patties. Fry in hot oil on both sides until golden brown. Top each burger with about 2 tablespoons of cheese as last side is cooking. Mix together mayonnaise and soy sauce, and spread on warm hamburger buns. Add a slice of tomato to each. These are also good cold for breakfast or lunch and without buns. Makes about 10 burgers.

ITALIAN MACARONI & CHEESE

Approximate cost: $3.20
Protein grams: 150
Preparation time: 50 minutes

Here's a high-protein quickie that appeals to the kids. Serve with Brown Rice Muffins (page 88) and a tossed green and carrot salad.

8

2	tablespoons oil	½	teaspoon dried basil
¾	cup finely chopped onion	¼	teaspoon pepper
¾	cup finely chopped celery	½	pound soy and whole-wheat (or whole-wheat) macaroni
1	clove garlic, mashed		
2	cans (6-ounce) tomato paste	⅔	cup grated Parmesan cheese
1½	cups water	1	pint (2 cups) cottage cheese
2	teaspoons salt		
½	teaspoon dried oregano		

Heat oil in frying pan, and sauté onion, celery, and garlic until softened. Stir in tomato paste, water, and seasonings. Simmer uncovered 5 minutes. Meanwhile, cook macaroni in boiling water. Rinse and drain. In a 2-quart casserole, make one layer of half the macaroni sprinkled with half the Parmesan cheese, half the cottage cheese, and half the sauce. Repeat for second layer, saving a little of the Parmesan cheese to top the sauce. Cover and bake in 350-degree oven for 30 to 35 minutes. Serves 4 to 5.

❛Hint: Uncooked pasta is not very fresh if it is crumbly or unusually brittle.❜

BEAN & RICE TACOS
Approximate cost: $2.80
Protein grams: 155
Preparation time: 35 minutes

These are tasty and easy to make. Serve them preceded by a cold soup (if you are really hungry) and followed by fresh fruit.

2½	cups cooked pink, pinto, or kidney beans, well drained	1	small onion, chopped Vinaigrette Dressing (page 79) or a little lemon juice
1½	cups cooked Brown Rice (page 102) Tomato or taco sauce or catsup Salt and pepper		
		1	dozen uncooked tortillas Oil for frying
1	large tomato, diced		
3	cups finely grated cabbage	2½	cups grated cheddar cheese

9

Combine beans and rice with just enough tomato or taco sauce (or a combination of both) to moisten mixture, and heat in saucepan. Salt and pepper to taste. Cover and keep warm. Mix together tomato, cabbage, and onion and dress lightly with vinaigrette or lemon juice. Fry tortillas, one at a time, in a little oil over a medium heat, bending each tortilla in half with a fork as you turn it. Fry until crisp. Absorb any excess oil between paper towels.

To assemble: In each tortilla, put a little of the bean-rice mixture, followed by a little of the cabbage. Top with cheese. Chopped cilantro (Chinese parsley) or chopped green chilis or avocados and sour cream are a nice optional touch. Makes 12 tacos.

●Hint: Cheese must be cooked over very low heat or it will become stringy and tough.●

TOMATO RAREBIT
Approximate cost (including bread): $4.50
Protein grams (including bread): 125
Preparation time: 25 minutes

This is an easy dish, and it has a lot of style.

3	large tomatoes, halved	¼	teaspoon salt
	Salt and pepper	1	pound sharp cheddar cheese, diced
2	tablespoons butter or margarine		
1	tablespoon Dijon mustard	½	cup beer
		2	egg yolks
½	teaspoon dry mustard	¼	cup light cream or evaporated milk
2	teaspoons Worcestershire sauce	6	slices Soy and Wheat-Sesame Bread, toasted (page 85)
½	teaspoon sweet paprika		

Preheat broiler. Salt and pepper tomato halves. Broil until tender, turning once to cook both sides. Keep tomatoes warm. Melt butter over very low heat in the top of double boiler; add mustards, Worcestershire sauce, paprika, and salt, and stir. (Water must be kept at a simmer as high heat will toughen cheese.) Add cheese, stirring frequently as it melts. Add beer, and continue to stir until cheese is completely melted. Beat egg yolks with cream, and add slowly to cheese mixture. Stir until thickened. Place warm tomatoes on toast, and spoon cheese over top. Serve immediately. Serves 6.

MOUSSAKA

Approximate cost: $3.25
Protein grams: 120
Preparation time (after eggplant is prepared): 1½ hours

This is a vegetarian version of the popular Middle Eastern dish of the same name. Serve with a tossed green salad and Soy and Wheat-Sesame Muffins (page 89).

1 medium eggplant, cut into ½-inch pieces	Salt
Salt	Cayenne pepper
2 medium onions, thinly sliced	2 large tomatoes, thinly sliced
3 cloves garlic, mashed	½ cup fresh minced parsley
3 tablespoons olive oil	½ teaspoon cinnamon
3 tablespoons butter or margarine	2 cups cooked bulgur wheat
3 tablespoons flour	2 cups grated mild white cheese
2 cups whole milk	½ cup grated Parmesan cheese

Sprinkle sliced eggplant with salt. Let drain on paper towels for an hour. Rinse and pat dry. Bake on lightly greased cookie sheet for 8 minutes in 375-degree oven. Meanwhile, sauté onions and garlic in oil until softened. In small saucepan make a white sauce: heat butter or margarine, and stir in flour; cook 5 minutes, stirring constantly. Add milk slowly, and stir until mixture thickens. Season to taste with salt and cayenne pepper, then set aside. In 8-by-12-inch casserole, layer half of eggplant slices followed by half of onion-and-garlic mixture. Over this spread half of sliced tomatoes. Mix together parsley, cinnamon, and bulgur wheat, and sprinkle half over casserole. Pour half the white sauce over the mixture, and sprinkle with half the white cheese. Repeat this entire process. Top with the Parmesan cheese. Cover and bake in 350-degree oven for 1 hour. Serves 6.

> ❢Hint: When you are making a white sauce, always cook the mixture well to get rid of the taste of raw flour.❢

ZUCCHINI PIZZA

Approximate cost: $3.60
Protein grams: 75
Preparation time: 45 to 50 minutes

Here's a good kids' dish, and as far as pizzas go, it is pretty low-calorie and high-nutrient. Serve with a fresh fruit salad.

3	cups grated zucchini	⅔	cup minced green onions
3	eggs, well beaten	½	cup minced pickled Italian peppers
⅓	cup unbleached flour	1	teaspoon dried oregano
¼	teaspoon salt	½	teaspoon dried basil
2	cups grated mozzarella cheese	2	medium tomatoes, thinly sliced
1	can (2¼-ounce) sliced black olives		

Press excess liquid from zucchini, and transfer to mixing bowl. Mix with eggs, flour, and salt. Spread into an oiled pizza pan, a 9-by-13-inch baking dish, or a cookie sheet with a lip. Bake in preheated, 450-degree oven for 8 minutes. Remove from oven and reduce heat to 350 degrees. Cover zucchini crust with cheese. Combine olives, onions, and peppers, and sprinkle over cheese. Sprinkle on herbs, and arrange tomato slices on top. Salt lightly, and return to oven for about 20 minutes, or until crust is set and cheese is melted. Serves 4 to 6.

BAKED ZUCCHINI FRITTATA

Approximate cost: $2.20
Protein grams: 80
Preparation time: 45 minutes

These next two zucchini recipes are for your summer cache, or for that year-round crop that seems to be increasingly available. Served cold, this is delicious picnic food. Serve with Soy and Wheat-Sesame Muffins (page 89) and sliced tomatoes.

2	tablespoons olive oil	8	eggs
3	cups sliced zucchini	⅔	cup grated Romano cheese
4	green onions, minced	1	teaspoon dried oregano
3	tablespoons fresh, minced parsley	¼	teaspoon salt
			Pepper

In frying pan, heat oil, and sauté zucchini, onions, and parsley until softened. Remove from heat. In mixing bowl beat eggs with cheese and seasonings. Add zucchini mixture, and blend well. Pour into lightly greased 9-inch-square baking pan, and bake in 350-degree oven for 25 minutes, or until set. Serve hot or cold. (Makes good picnic food.) Serves 6.

CALIFORNIA VEGETABLE QUICHE

Approximate cost: $2.50
Protein grams: 90
Preparation time: 45 to 50 minutes

This is an old favorite from my first cookbook. It allows for great variation and unlimited creativity. I suggest serving with any cooked grain, sliced tomatoes, and raw carrot and celery sticks.

1	pound summer squash, green or yellow	1	teaspoon any dried herb (dill, basil, oregano, or tarragon)
4	eggs, beaten		
2	cups grated Swiss or Monterey Jack cheese	1½	teaspoons salt
		¼	cup grated Parmesan cheese

Steam squash until tender. Mash well with potato masher, and drain off excess liquid.

OR

Grate squash coarsely into a bowl. Sprinkle lightly with salt, and let it sit 10 minutes. Squeeze out all liquid.

In large mixing bowl, mix prepared squash, beaten eggs, cheese, and seasonings. Pour in greased, 8-inch-square baking dish, and top with Parmesan cheese. Bake in 350-degree oven for 30 to 40 minutes, or until a knife inserted in center comes out clean and edges are slightly golden. Serves 4 to 5.

CHEESE & SQUASH PILAF

Approximate cost: $2.15
Protein grams: 80
Preparation time: 30 minutes

Another good summer squash recipe! Serve with coleslaw and fresh fruit.

1 **medium onion, finely chopped**	½ **teaspoon salt**
1 **cup uncooked bulgur wheat**	½ **teaspoon pepper**
2 **tablespoons butter or margarine**	1 **can (8-ounce) tomato sauce**
2 **cups vegetable stock (use vegetable bouillon cubes)**	3 **cups thinly sliced summer squash (any variety)**
1 **teaspoon dried oregano**	1½ **cups ricotta cheese**
	½ **cup grated Parmesan cheese**

In large frying pan, sauté onions and bulgur wheat in butter or margarine for about 4 to 5 minutes. Add stock and seasonings, and cover. Simmer for 15 to 18 minutes, or until liquid is absorbed. Stir in tomato sauce and squash, and simmer, covered, until squash is tender. Spread ricotta cheese over, and sprinkle with Parmesan cheese. Cover and simmer until dish is bubbly. Serves 5 to 6.

●Hint: Many natural cheeses, including Swiss and cheddar, can be frozen. They should be well wrapped.●

SWISS ONION QUICHE

Approximate cost (including pie shell): $2.50
Protein grams (including pie shell): 100
Preparation time (including pie shell preparation): 50 minutes

A great, easy light supper dish. Serve with mixed vegetable salad and fresh fruit.

3	tablespoons butter or margarine	1	cup light cream (half-and-half)
2	large onions, thinly sliced	½	teaspoon salt
		½	teaspoon nutmeg
2	cups grated Swiss cheese, packed	1	single unbaked pie shell (page 96)
3	large eggs		

In a Dutch oven, heat butter or margarine, and sauté onions until well softened and golden, about 15 to 20 minutes. Meanwhile, grate cheese. Beat eggs with cream, salt, and nutmeg. Spread onions at bottom of unbaked pie shell, and cover with cheese. Pour egg mixture over this, and put into preheated 375-degree oven for 25 to 30 minutes, or until a knife inserted in the center comes out clean and top is slightly golden. Serve warm. Serves 6.

●Hint: Undiluted canned skimmed milk is a good low-calorie substitute for cream in cooking and sauces.●

PUREED VEGETABLE SOUP
Approximate cost (not including sandwiches): $.75
Protein grams (not including sandwiches): 15
Preparation time(unless chilled): 20 minutes

This simple but delicious soup can be served hot or cold. Serve with grilled cheese sandwiches made with Soy and Wheat-Sesame Bread (page 85) and with apples.

1	medium zucchini	1	quart water
2	medium potatoes, peeled	1	teaspoon dill
		1	tablespoon olive oil (optional)
1	medium onion		Salt and pepper
2	large carrots		

Chop vegetables coarsely, and put into soup pot with water. Bring to a boil, and reduce heat. Cover and simmer for 10 minutes. Transfer a little at a time to blender, and blend until smooth. Return to pot, and stir in dill and olive oil. Salt and pepper to taste. Serve hot or cold. Serves 4 to 5.

Note: This type of soup can be made with any combination of vegetables, and it can be made thicker or thinner, depending on your preference. For maximum nutrition serve with cheese sandwiches as suggested, or in the winter, hot corn bread, cheese, and apples are a nice combination.

VEGETABLE CURRY
Approximate cost (including rice): $2.30
Protein grams (including rice): 65
Preparation time: 50 minutes

Serve with a tossed green salad. If you are feeling more extravagant, you can serve this with condiments such as peanuts, raisins, shredded coconut, chutney, etc.

3 tablespoons oil	½ cup green pepper
1 large onion, finely chopped	½ cup celery
	1 cup sliced mushrooms
1 large apple, peeled, cored, and grated	1 cup unflavored yogurt
1 large carrot, grated	
2 cloves garlic, grated	1 tablespoon lemon juice
1 tablespoon flour	1 tablespoon honey
1 cup rich vegetable broth (use bouillon cubes)	Salt
	Crushed, dried chili peppers
2 teaspoons curry powder	5 to 6 cups cooked Brown Rice (page 102)
½ teaspoon cumin	
1½ cups chopped string beans	3 tablespoons toasted sesame seeds
2 cups chopped zucchini	

Heat oil in large frying pan, and sauté onion, apple, carrot, and garlic until softened. Stir in flour, vegetable broth, and seasonings; simmer, covered, for 30 minutes. Add remaining vegetables, cover, and simmer until vegetables are tender but not mushy. Remove from heat and stir in yogurt, lemon juice, and honey. Add salt and pepper and crushed, dried chili peppers to taste. Serve over brown rice, and garnish with toasted sesame seeds. Serves 5 to 6.

❦Hint: To thicken sauce and keep it clear, use arrowroot, cornstarch, or potato starch.❧

❧TOFU DISHES☙

The next six recipes use tofu as the main ingredient. Tofu is the cheese or curd made from soybeans that is a traditional staple of Asian cooking. As it becomes more available on this continent, it is being used in western-style dishes. Tofu is an excellent source of usable protein, and it is high in calcium. It also contains a fair amount of iron, potassium, phosphorous, sodium, and B vitamins. Tofu is easily digested, but because of its mild taste it should be cooked with other flavorful ingredients. Packaged in sealed, plastic boxes, tofu can be found in the produce or dairy sections of supermarkets or Asian markets. Try sneaking tofu into other casserole dishes; it adds texture and does not alter the taste if used in small amounts. It certainly adds nutrients to anyone's diet.

VEGETABLE TOFU SAUTÉ

Approximate cost: $2
Protein grams: 30
Preparation time: 20 minutes

This is good for brunch, lunch, or dinner. Serve with brown rice and a tomato and onion salad.

½ pound tofu	1 cup chopped broccoli
3 tablespoons soy sauce	1 cup grated carrots
¼ teaspoon powdered cumin	1 cup chopped mushrooms
¼ teaspoon powdered ginger	½ cup fresh, minced parsley
3 tablespoons oil	¼ teaspoon thyme
½ cup chopped green onions	2 to 3 tablespoons toasted sesame seeds (optional)
½ cup chopped celery	
2 cloves garlic	

Slice tofu in ½-inch thick slices and lay in a shallow pan or plate. Mix together soy sauce, cumin, and ginger and pour over tofu. Turn each piece to cover with mixture.

In a frying pan, heat oil and sauté onions and celery with garlic to soften, for a couple of minutes. Add broccoli and carrots and continue to sauté for 4 to 5 minutes more, then stir in mushrooms, parsley, and thyme. Continue to cook over low heat for several minutes to soften, then add tofu slices. (Retain sauce.) Cook all ingredients so that tofu is well heated. (Be careful not to break up tofu too much.) Add remaining sauce to taste and salt to taste. Top with toasted sesame seeds if desired. Serves 4.

Note: To toast sesame seeds, sprinkle raw seeds in a shallow oven dish and toast in a 300-degree oven until lightly browned.

EGGPLANT TOFU PARMESAN

Approximate cost: $5
Protein grams: 125
Preparation time: 1 hour

This is a good company dish. Serve with a green salad and Soy and Wheat-Sesame Muffins (page 89).

SAUCE:

¼	cup oil	½	teaspoon basil
1	cup chopped onion	½	teaspoon oregano
2	cloves garlic, mashed	2	cans (15-ounce) tomato sauce
⅓	cup chopped parsley	½	pound tofu
			Salt and pepper

EGGPLANT:

	Oil		Flour
2	medium to small eggplants, unpeeled		Salt
		1	cup Parmesan cheese
2	to 3 eggs, beaten	½	pound mozzarella

To prepare sauce: Heat oil in large frying pan and sauté onions and garlic with parsley until softened. Stir in seasonings. Put 1 can of tomato sauce in blender with tofu and blend until smooth. Add to sauteéd onions with second can of tomato sauce. Simmer, uncovered, for 8 to 10 minutes and salt and pepper to taste.

To prepare eggplant: In another frying pan put 2 tablespoons oil. Slice eggplant into ½-inch slices, dip in egg and lightly flour. Fry 2 to 3 slices at a time (2 to 3 minutes on each side), salting each piece lightly. Add 2 more tablespoons oil and repeat process until all slices are fried. In a 9-by-13-inch baking pan spread a thin layer of sauce and then cover with a layer of eggplant. Sprinkle ½ of Parmesan over top and then spoon over half of remaining sauce. Follow this with another layer of eggplant, the remaining Parmesan cheese, and the remaining sauce. Cover with slices of mozzarella cheese. Cover with foil. Bake in 350-degree oven for about 25 minutes. Serves 6 generously.

TOFU & SPINACH-STUFFED MANICOTTI

Approximate cost: $3
Protein grams: 60
Preparation time: 50 minutes

In this recipe, the tofu tastes like ricotta cheese. Serve with steamed carrots or yellow squash and Soy and Wheat-Sesame Bread (p. 85).

8 manicotti (pasta) shells	Boiling water

FILLING:

¼ cup minced onion	½ teaspoon dried oregano
2 tablespoons oil	
1 tablespoon fresh, minced parsley	1 pound fresh tofu
1 large clove garlic, mashed	1 package (10-ounce) frozen spinach, thawed
½ teaspoon dried basil	1 egg, beaten
	Salt and pepper

SAUCE:

3 large tomatoes	Salt
2 teaspoons oil	
½ teaspoon dried basil	⅓ cup grated Parmesan cheese
½ teaspoon dried thyme	

Cook manicotti according to directions on package. Drain and cool slightly.

To prepare filling: Sauté onion in oil until softened, and add parsley, garlic, basil, and oregano as it is cooking. In mixing bowl, mash tofu with a potato masher, and stir in spinach from

19

which excess water has been squeezed. Stir in onion mixture and egg. Mix well, and add salt and pepper to taste.

To prepare sauce: Peel tomatoes and mince. Put in saucepan with oil, basil, and thyme. Cook, uncovered, over medium heat until well blended and thickened, about 10 minutes. Salt to taste.

To assemble: While sauce is cooking, stuff cooled manicotti shells with tofu mixture and place shells close together in shallow baking pan. Pour sauce over this, and sprinkle with grated Parmesan cheese. Cover and put in 350-degree oven for about 20 minutes. Serve immediately. Serves 4 to 6.

TOFUBURGERS
Approximate cost: $1.70
Protein grams: 65
Preparation time: 20 to 25 minutes

Serve with Brown Rice (p. 102), coleslaw, and a yellow vegetable, if desired.

1 **pound fresh tofu**	¼ **cup unbleached flour**
1 **egg, beaten**	
2 **tablespoons oil**	1 **teaspoon salt**
⅓ **cup minced green onion**	½ **teaspoon oregano**
	½ **teaspoon basil**
2 **cloves garlic, mashed**	½ **cup raw wheat germ**
½ **cup minced celery**	⅓ **cup grated Romano cheese**
3 **tablespoons fresh, minced parsley**	**Oil for frying**
	Chopped tomatoes

Beat tofu and egg together in mixing bowl. Heat oil in large skillet over medium heat; add onion, garlic, celery, and parsley, and sauté until limp. Stir onion mixture into tofu mixture. Add flour, salt, and seasonings. Combine wheat germ, cheese, and seasonings in a bowl. Shape tofu mixture into 6 patties. (The mixture will be very soft, so handle it carefully.) Coat patties with wheat germ-and-cheese mixture, and fry in hot oil, turning once, so both sides are golden brown. Garnish with chopped tomatoes. Serves 4 to 6.

❧FROZEN TOFU DISHES❧

The next two recipes are made with tofu that has been frozen and thawed. It has a consistency somewhat like ground meat. Freeze tofu in the package in which you buy it. After 4 to 5 days, thaw it at room temperature, press out excess liquid, and crumble the thawed tofu with your fingers. Use immediately or return to the refrigerator and use very soon.

TOFU NOODLE HASH
Approximate cost: $2.50
Protein grams: 90
Preparation time: 35 minutes

Serve with a tossed greens-and-carrot salad.

¼ cup oil	2 vegetable bouillon cubes
1 small onion, finely chopped	¼ cup boiling water
½ green pepper, finely chopped	2 teaspoons sweet paprika
½ red pepper, finely chopped	¼ teaspoon dried thyme
2 cups finely shredded green cabbage	3 cups cooked soy-and-wheat noodles
2 cloves garlic, mashed	1 can (1-pound) tomatoes
8 ounces tofu, frozen, thawed, squeezed, and crumbled	Salt and pepper
	1 cup grated mild white cheese
	1 cup sour cream

In a large pot or Dutch oven, heat oil, and sauté onion and peppers until softened. Add cabbage and garlic, and cook another 4 to 5 minutes, stirring frequently. Stir in tofu. Dissolve bouillon cubes in boiling water, and add to pot, along with paprika and thyme. Stir in noodles and tomatoes. Use fork or spatula to break tomatoes. Simmer, covered, for 15 minutes. Salt and pepper to taste, and sprinkle cheese over top. Let cheese melt and stir in sour cream just before serving. Serves 4 to 6.

21

SPICY TOFU RICE
Approximate cost: $2.80
Protein grams: 75
Preparation time: 35 minutes

Serve with a tossed green salad or coleslaw and perhaps a steamed yellow vegetable.

⅓ cup oil	1 teaspoon salt
1 small onion, chopped	2 teaspoons powdered vegetable bouillon
⅔ cup chopped green pepper	1 can (2¼-ounce) sliced black olives
⅔ cup chopped celery	3 cups cooked Brown Rice (page 102)
2 cloves garlic, mashed	1 can (1-pound) stewed tomatoes
8 ounces tofu, frozen, thawed, and crumbled	1½ cups grated, sharp cheddar cheese
½ teaspoon dried thyme	
1 generous teaspoon chili powder	

Heat oil in deep frying pan, and sauté onion, pepper, celery, and garlic until softened. Add tofu, seasonings, and bouillon. Stir in olives and brown rice. Purée tomatoes in blender and add to frying pan. Simmer, uncovered, for about 15 minutes, until liquid is absorbed. The rice should not be dry, but neither should it be soupy. Sprinkle cheese over top, and cover pan and cook until it is melted. Serves 4 to 6.

MEAT DISHES

Although more and more meals are planned around non-meat protein these days, meat is still the major protein source in this country. It is also the most expensive. On the other hand, our reliance on fast-foods—at its height in this past decade—has shrunk the food dollar more than any other factor. When you feel distressed about the price of a roast, bear in mind that it is not much more than the cost of a large pizza prepared for you.

The recipes in this section are confined to the least expensive cuts and they have been prepared with an eye to stretching meat, especially ground meat, whether it be beef, pork, lamb, or veal. Fortunately, the recent interest in international recipes has taught us that meat can be used to augment a dish rather than as the main ingredient.

Ground beef is the most popular meat these days, although I offer a number of recipes using bulk sausage because pork is less expensive than beef and is also a good source of B vitamins. In small quantities, country-style pork sausage is a good flavoring in a dish. Because pork is high in fat, it is important to render, or liquefy, the fat by cooking; it can then be drained off. Pork always should be cooked thoroughly. This does not mean, however, that pork has to be cooked at a high temperature. In fact, all meat should be cooked at low temperatures to keep the protein fibers from becoming tough. This also saves energy.

Finally, several recipes using liver are included because it is still reasonably priced, and because it is also a good source of B vitamins. Of all the variety meats, it is the most widely available.

MEATLOAF À LA WELLINGTON

Approximate cost: $5.75
Protein grams: 190
Preparation time: 1½ hours

This is good company fare topped with horseradish-sour cream. Serve with sautéed, herbed carrots and string beans and a green salad with Mustard Dressing (p. 80).

MEATLOAF:

1½	pounds lean ground beef	½	cup finely chopped onion
2	eggs	⅓	cup finely grated carrot
⅓	cup catsup	1½	teaspoons salt
2	teaspoons Worcestershire sauce	¼	teaspoon dried thyme
1	cup soft, fresh bread crumbs	¼	teaspoon nutmeg
4	teaspoons butter or margarine	⅛	teaspoon pepper
		½	pound fresh mushrooms, sliced

PASTRY:

2	cups unbleached flour	⅓	cup well chilled butter
1	scant teaspoon salt	⅓	cup shortening
¼	teaspoon thyme	⅓	cup ice water

SAUCE:

1 cup sour cream
with 2 teaspoons
freshly prepared
horseradish

To prepare meatloaf: Break up meat with a large fork in a large mixing bowl. In a smaller bowl, beat eggs with catsup and Worcestershire sauce; mix in bread crumbs and set aside. Heat 3 teaspoons butter or margarine in a small frying pan, and sauté onion and carrot until softened and then combine meat and bread-crumb mixture, and add salt, thyme, nutmeg, and pepper. Beat mixture with a large fork until well mixed. Set aside. Heat remaining teaspoon butter or margarine in same frying pan, and sauté mushrooms until just slightly softened. Salt lightly and set aside.

To make pastry: Combine flour with salt and thyme in a large mixing bowl. Cut in butter and shortening with a pastry blender or fork until mixture resembles coarse meal. Stir in ice water with a few quick strokes, enough to hold dough together. On a lightly floured board or pastry marble, roll out ⅓ of the dough about ⅛-inch thick. Trim to make an 8-by-12-inch rectangle. Transfer to a lightly oiled cookie sheet. Roll out remaining dough ⅛-inch thick.

To assemble dish: Place ⅔ of meat mixture in a loaf shape on top of pastry on cookie sheet. Leave enough dough exposed around all four sides so you can crimp together with top layer of dough. Make a long indentation in the top of the meat and fill with the mushrooms. Cover with remaining meat mixture. Gently lift remaining dough, and cover the meat mixture. Trim away excess dough, and crimp edges of two layers of dough together. Roll out remaining dough, and cut into flower and leaf shapes to decorate the top of the pastry. Bake in 350-degree, preheated oven for 1 hour, or until pastry is golden brown. Let cool 5 minutes before slicing.

To make sauce: Mix sour cream with horseradish and serve in separate bowl. Serves 6 to 8.

STOVE BARBECUED BEEF
Approximate cost (not including buns): $2.90
Protein grams (not including buns): 100
Preparation time: 25 minutes

Serve over Whole-wheat Hamburger Buns (page 86) and with a mixed green salad.

2 tablespoons oil	**1 teaspoon sweet paprika**
1 small onion, finely chopped	**1 teaspoon chili powder**
1 pound lean ground beef	**½ teaspoon cinnamon**
1 can (8-ounce) tomato sauce	**¼ teaspoon black pepper**
2 tablespoons Worcestershire sauce	**¼ teaspoon ground cloves**
¼ cup dry red wine	**1 tablespoon brown sugar or molasses**
1 teaspoon salt	

Heat oil and sauté onion until softened. Add beef and brown as onions continue cooking. Stir in remaining ingredients, cover, and simmer for about 15 minutes. Serves 4 to 5.

BEEF & VEGETABLE LOAF
Approximate cost: $2.75
Protein grams: 120
Preparation time: 1 hour, 15 minutes

Serve with baked winter squash (or summer squash when in season) and sliced tomatoes.

½	medium onion, finely chopped	¾	cup soft bread crumbs
2	tablespoons oil	¼	cup evaporated milk
1	cup finely chopped cabbage	1	pound lean ground beef
2	tablespoons fresh, minced parsley	¼	teaspoon dried thyme
1	small potato, peeled and coarsely grated	¼	teaspoon nutmeg
2	cloves garlic, mashed	1	teaspoon salt
			Pepper

In a frying pan, sauté onion in oil. Meanwhile, soak bread crumbs in milk. When onion begins to soften, add cabbage, parsley, potato, and garlic. In a medium-sized bowl, combine sautéed ingredients, bread crumbs, beef, and seasonings and mix well. Shape into a loaf, and place in a shallow baking dish or loaf pan. Bake in 350-degree oven for approximately 1 hour. Let cool a few minutes before slicing. Serves 5 to 6.

Note: Beating ground meat mixtures with a large fork is tenderizing whereas working it with your hands tends to toughen the meat.

BEEF & BARLEY LOAF
Approximate cost: $1.75
Protein grams: 75
Preparation time: 1 hour

Serve with a cabbage salad and applesauce.

2	cups finely grated carrots	1	egg
1	small onion, minced	¼	cup evaporated milk
1	cup cooked barley	¼	cup catsup
¼	cup fine, dry bread crumbs	½	teaspoon salt
½	pound lean ground beef	¼	teaspoon nutmeg
		¼	teaspoon thyme

In a large bowl, combine carrots, onion, barley, and bread crumbs. Stir in beef with a large fork. Beat together egg, milk, and catsup, and add to beef mixture with seasonings. Shape into a loaf, and bake in a 350-degree oven for about 45 to 50 minutes. Serves 4 to 6.

PORCUPINE MEATBALLS
Approximate cost: $3.25
Protein grams: 115
Preparation time: 1 hour, 15 minutes

These were a great favorite in my family—and they are very easy to make. Serve with coleslaw.

1	pound lean ground beef	1	can (1-pound 12-ounce) whole tomatoes with liquid
1	egg, beaten	2	cups water
½	cup milk	2	tablespoons minced onion
⅔	cup uncooked brown rice	½	teaspoon dried basil
½	teaspoon chili powder		Salt
¼	teaspoon cumin	1	tablespoon cornstarch
1½	teaspoons salt		

In a bowl, combine meat, egg, milk, rice, chili powder, cumin, and salt. Beat together with a large fork until well blended. Set aside. In a large pot, combine tomatoes and their liquid, water, onion, and basil. Salt lightly. Bring mixture to a boil, then reduce heat to simmer. Shape meatballs into 18 to 20 balls, and drop in simmering sauce. Cover and cook for about 1½ hours, or until rice is tender. Remove the meatballs from the sauce with a slotted spoon. Mix cornstarch with a little cold water, and add to sauce. Cook to thicken slightly. Serve meatballs and sauce in shallow bowls. Serves 4 to 5.

❥Hint: Add a little cold water or evaporated milk to ground beef to make a grilled hamburger juicier.❥

JOE'S SPECIAL
Approximate cost: $3
Protein grams: 130
Preparation time: 20 minutes

Here's a wonderful stew concoction—famous in San Francisco but certain to be popular anywhere, and easy to prepare. Serve with a tomato salad, raw carrot sticks, and hot French bread.

2	tablespoons oil	½	teaspoon dried basil
1	pound lean ground beef	½	teaspoon marjoram
1	small onion, minced	1	teaspoon salt Pepper
1	package (10-ounce) frozen, chopped spinach, thawed and squeezed of excess liquid	4	large eggs

Heat oil in heavy frying pan, and brown meat and cook onion until softened. Stir in spinach and seasonings. Beat eggs and add to meat mixture. Stir until eggs are set. Serves 4 to 5.

CHILI CON CARNÉ
Approximate cost: $3.80
Protein grams: 98
Preparation time: 1 hour, 10 minutes

This is an easy, hearty recipe that is quite spicy, but you can modify the seasonings to your taste. Serve with Corn Muffins (page 88) and a green salad with carrots.

½ pound lean ground beef
½ pound bulk pork sausage
2 large onions, chopped
3 cloves garlic, minced
1 medium green pepper, seeded and chopped
1 can (1-pound 12-ounce) tomatoes with liquid
4 teaspoons chili powder
1 teaspoon dried oregano
½ teaspoon cumin
½ teaspoon crushed, dried red peppers
2 cans (15-ounce each) pink or pinto beans with liquid
Salt

In a Dutch oven, brown beef and sausage with onions, garlic, and pepper. When vegetables are softened, drain off any excess fat, and add tomatoes, seasonings, and beans. Bring to a boil, then reduce heat. Salt to taste, and simmer for 40 minutes. Add water to achieve desired consistency as it cooks. Serves 5 to 6.

●Hint: Tea is a good tenderizer. Use it instead of water in stews and for braising.●

ENCHILADA STACK
Approximate cost: $5
Protein grams: 160
Preparation time: 40 minutes

This is an easy, much-enjoyed special for Mexican food fans. Serve with a tossed green salad and with Guacamole (page 106) when avocados are in season.

2 tablespoons vegetable oil
1 pound lean ground beef
1 medium onion, finely chopped
1 cup finely shredded carrots
2 cloves garlic, mashed
1 can (2¼-ounce) sliced black olives, drained
½ teaspoon salt
¼ teaspoon pepper
1 can (10-ounce) enchilada sauce
1 can (8-ounce) tomato sauce
⅓ cup water
8 corn tortillas
1 package (3½-ounce) cream cheese, softened
2 cups shredded cheddar cheese

Heat oil in heavy frying pan, and brown meat and cook onion until softened. Add carrots and garlic, and cook 2 to 3 more minutes. Mix in olives, salt, pepper, enchilada sauce, and water to make a thick sauce. Spread 6 tortillas with cream cheese. Place 2 tortillas side by side in a shallow baking pan. Top with ⅓ of the meat sauce, and cover them with ¼ of the cheddar cheese. Repeat 2 times. Top with remaining 2 tortillas and cover with remaining cheddar cheese. Sprinkle 2 to 3 tablespoons of water over both stacks and cover. Bake in 350-degree oven for about 20 minutes. Serves 5 to 6.

QUICK TAMALE PIE

Approximate cost: $4
Protein grams: 145
Preparation time: 1 hour, 10 minutes

Serve with a tossed green salad and raw carrots.

FILLING:

2 tablespoons oil
1 pound lean ground beef
1 medium onion, chopped
2 cloves garlic, mashed
1 can (1-pound) stewed tomatoes
1 cup sweet corn, fresh, frozen, or canned
1 can (3¼ ounce) pitted, black olives, drained and halved
1 to 2 teaspoons chili powder, to taste
½ teaspoon cumin Salt

TOPPING:

3 cups cold water	½ teaspoon salt
1½ cups yellow corn meal	⅔ cup grated cheddar cheese
½ teaspoon chili powder	

To prepare filling: Heat oil in heavy frying pan, and brown meat with onion and garlic. Stir in stewed tomatoes, corn, olives, chili powder, and cumin. Simmer 5 minutes, and add salt to taste.

To prepare topping: Put water, corn meal, chili powder, and salt in a saucepan; cook over high heat, stirring constantly. You must stir constantly for 8 to 10 minutes or it will stick or burn.

To assemble pie: Grease an 8-inch-square pan, and spread ½ of corn mixture on the bottom. Pour in meat mixture, and spread remaining corn mixture over this. Bake in a 350-degree preheated oven for about 40 minutes, or until top is set. Sprinkle cheese over top during the last few minutes. Serves 5 to 6.

GROUND BEEF MINESTRONE
Approximate cost: $4
Protein grams: 183
Preparation time: 45 minutes

This is a quick and tasty winter soup. Serve followed by a tossed green salad and hot bread.

1 pound lean ground meat	1 package (10-ounce) frozen mixed vegetables
2 cloves garlic, minced	1 can (15-ounce) kidney beans
1 large onion, finely chopped	1 teaspoon dried oregano
1 can (1-pound 12-ounce) whole tomatoes	1 teaspoon dried basil
1 quart beef stock	½ teaspoon dried thyme
1 cup uncooked macaroni	½ cup dry red wine
1 medium zucchini, diced	Salt and pepper
	Grated Parmesan or Romano cheese

In a heavy soup pot, brown beef and cook garlic and onion until soft. Add tomatoes, and bring to a boil. Reduce heat and simmer for 15 minutes, breaking them up with a fork. Add stock and bring to a boil. Add macaroni. Cook over low heat for 10 minutes, then add zucchini, vegetables, beans, seasonings, and wine. Cover and simmer for 10 minutes. Salt and pepper to taste. Serve with grated cheese on the side. Serves 5 to 6.

❝Hint: Ground meat does not keep as long as whole cuts.❞

GROUND BEEF & CABBAGE STEW
Approximate cost: $3.50
Protein grams: 155
Preparation time: 45 minutes

Serve with boiled potatoes and steamed carrots.

2	tablespoons oil	½	cup unflavored yogurt
1	pound lean ground beef	2	cloves garlic, mashed
1	cup chopped onion	½	teaspoon dried basil
1	cup chopped celery	½	teaspoon dried oregano
½	large cabbage	½	teaspoon dried thyme
	Salt	1	cup grated mozzarella cheese
1	can (8-ounce) tomato sauce		

In a deep frying pan, brown meat in oil with onions and celery. Cut cabbage lengthwise into thick slices, and lay across meat. Remove from heat, and salt mixture lightly. Mix together tomato sauce, yogurt, garlic, and herbs, and pour over meat-and-cabbage mixture. Cover and put into a preheated, 350-degree oven for about 20 to 25 minutes. Cabbage should be tender, but not mushy. Sprinkle with cheese last few minutes of cooking. Serves 4 to 6.

❝Hint: Place a couple of bay leaves in the bottom of the pan when you roast beef to add flavor and aroma.❞

BEEF & VEGETABLE SPAGHETTI SAUCE

Approximate cost (not including pasta): $3.70
Protein grams (not including pasta): 85
Preparation time: 1 hour, 45 minutes

This is a hearty meal with a tossed green salad and French bread. The leftovers are good when mixed with cooked spaghetti, baked, and topped with a little cheese.

1 large onion, minced	¼ teaspoon cinnamon
3 tablespoons oil	¼ teaspoon dried
3 cloves garlic,	thyme
minced	Salt
2 tablespoons fresh,	¾ pound lean ground
minced parsley	beef
2 cans (15-ounce	1 large carrot,
each) Italian plum	coarsely grated
tomatoes	1 medium zucchini,
1 can (6-ounce)	diced
tomato paste with 1	1 cup shredded
can water	cabbage
1 bay leaf	Hot cooked pasta
½ teaspoon dried	Grated Parmesan
oregano	cheese

Sauté onion in oil in a deep, heavy frying pan or Dutch oven. As it softens, add garlic and parsley, and continue to sauté. Add tomatoes, tomato paste, water, bay leaf, oregano, cinnamon, and thyme. Bring to a boil; reduce heat, and salt to taste. Cover and simmer for about 40 minutes, or until well blended. Brown beef in a separate pan and add to sauce. Add vegetables and continue to simmer, uncovered, about 35 to 40 minutes, until sauce thickens slightly. Serve over hot pasta with grated Parmesan cheese. Serves 5 to 6.

❦Hint: Always use variety meats soon after you
purchase them. They do not keep well, nor do
they freeze all that well.❧

BRAISED LAMB SHANKS & VEGETABLES

Approximate cost: $5
Protein grams: 180
Preparation time: 2 hours

Watch for a special on lamb shanks. The meat is sweet near the bone, and this is a good one-dish meal you can serve with or without a salad.

- **3 to 4 lamb shanks, cracked**
- **Flour**
- **3 tablespoons oil**
- **Salt and pepper**
- **⅔ cup hot water or beef broth**
- **2 large cloves garlic, minced**
- **1 bay leaf**
- **4 large carrots, halved**
- **4 large potatoes, peeled and halved**
- **½ teaspoon dried thyme**
- **½ teaspoon dried rosemary**
- **⅓ cup dry red wine**
- **½ cabbage**

Sprinkle lamb shanks with flour. In a large Dutch oven, heat oil over a medium heat. Brown lamb well on all sides; salt and pepper lightly, and reduce heat to simmer. Add water or broth, garlic, and bay leaf. Cover and simmer for 40 minutes. Add more water if necessary, but keep water level low so meat is braised. Remove from heat, and add a little water to the bottom of the pan; add carrots and potatoes. Sprinkle with thyme and rosemary, and add salt and pepper again. Add wine, and cover tightly. Put in 300-degree oven for 40 to 60 minutes, or until meat and vegetables are tender. Cut cabbage in quarters and add last 20 minutes. Salt lightly. (Cabbage should be crunchy but tender.) Serves 4.

Hint: Add a little grated raw potato to a meatloaf, meatballs, or hamburger mixture to add juiciness and act as a binder.

DILLED LAMB MEATBALLS
Approximate cost: $3.50
Protein grams: 80
Preparation time: 1 hour

Serve with Bulgur Wheat (page 103) and steamed spinach and carrots.

1 **pound ground lamb**	½ **cup grated**
2 **cups soft bread**	**Parmesan cheese**
crumbs	1 **teaspoon salt**
½ **cup minced green**	1½ **teaspoons dried dill**
onion	1 **egg, beaten**
2 **cloves garlic,**	2 **tablespoons oil**
mashed	½ **cup sour cream**
	½ **cup unflavored**
	yogurt

Mix together lamb, bread crumbs, onion, garlic, cheese, salt, and 1 teaspoon of the dill. Stir with a fork to combine all ingredients well, then stir in egg. Shape into 16 to 18 small balls, and brown well in oil over medium heat. Reduce heat and drain off any grease. Combine yogurt and sour cream with remaining dill, and spoon over meatballs; cover and simmer for 30 minutes. Serves 5 to 6.

PORK ROAST IN BEER
Approximate cost: $5
Protein grams: 185 to 260
Preparation time: 3 to 4 hours

Serve with Oven Fries (page 104), steamed carrots, and coleslaw.

3 **to 4 pound pork**	½ **teaspoon dried**
shoulder roast	**rosemary**
3 **large cloves garlic,**	½ **teaspoon dried**
slivered	**thyme**
3 **medium onions,**	1 **cup dark beer**
thinly sliced	**Salt and pepper**
Salt	
3 **soda crackers**	

Make little cuts in pork with sharp knife point, and insert garlic slivers in roast. In a Dutch oven, brown meat lightly in its own fat over low-medium heat. Remove pork, and sauté onions in pork fat. (It may be necessary to add a little oil.) Salt onions lightly.

36

Return pork to pot, and cover with onions. Roll soda crackers into crumbs, and mix with rosemary and thyme. Combine with beer, and pour over pork. Salt and pepper lightly. Cover tightly, and roast in a 325-degree, preheated oven for 2½ to 3½ hours. (Cook approximately 35 minutes per pound; the internal temperature when done should be 185° F.) Serves 5 to 6.

HAM HOCK & SPLIT PEA SOUP

Approximate cost: $2.80
Protein grams: 250
Preparation time: 2 hours

Use a meaty ham bone, or watch for a special on ham hocks. Serve with Corn Muffins (page 88) and apple quarters.

- **2 cups green split peas**
- **2 quarts water or vegetable stock**
- **1 meaty ham bone or 1- to 2-pound ham hock**
- **1 large onion, finely chopped**
- **2 large carrots, halved and thinly sliced**
- **2 ribs celery, chopped**
- **2 fresh tomatoes, cored, peeled and chopped (optional when expensive)**
- **3 cloves garlic, mashed**
- **½ teaspoon dried thyme**
- **½ teaspoon dried basil**
- **1½ teaspoon salt**
- **2 to 3 tablespoons white or cider vinegar**

Rinse peas. Bring water or stock to a boil in large soup pan or Dutch oven. Pour peas in, and reduce heat to simmer. Cover and cook for 45 to 50 minutes, or until peas soften. Add ham bone, onion, carrots, celery, tomatoes, garlic, and seasonings. Salt to taste. Continue to simmer, covered, for another hour, and add water to desired consistency. Add vinegar 15 minutes before serving. Serves 4 to 6.

PORK CHOPS & CHEESE POTATOES

Approximate cost: $4.60
Protein grams: 130
Preparation time: 1 hour, 10 minutes

Serve with a steamed yellow vegetable and coleslaw.

4 pork chops	**4 to 5 medium**
½ teaspoon dried	**potatoes**
rosemary	**⅓ cup milk**
Salt and pepper	**⅓ cup grated Romano**
1 tablespoon oil	**or Parmesan**
1 medium onion,	**cheese**
thinly sliced	**Sweet paprika**

Trim pork chops, and melt fat in a heavy frying pan. Brown pork chops slowly on both sides. Sprinkle with rosemary, and salt and pepper lightly. Transfer to a shallow casserole dish. Remove any fat scraps from pan and heat oil. Sauté onion slices over low heat until softened. Meanwhile, peel and cut potatoes into very thin slices. Arrange sliced potatoes on top of chops, and cover with onion slices. Salt and pepper lightly, and pour milk over top. Sprinkle with grated cheese and paprika. Bake in a 375-degree preheated oven for about 45 minutes, or until potatoes are tender and pork is cooked through. Serves 4.

●Hint: If you grind pork at home, be sure that you wash grinder parts very well afterward. Scald them if you can.●

SAUSAGE CABBAGE ROLLS

Approximate cost: $3.20
Protein grams: 75
Preparation time: 1 hour, 10 minutes

This is an economical and interesting company dish. Serve with a raw vegetable platter and hot Corn Muffins (page 88).

1 large head green cabbage

SAUCE:

1   small onion, thinly
    sliced
3   tablespoons oil
4   to 5 medium
    tomatoes, peeled
    and chopped
1   cup hot water
1   vegetable bouillon
    cube

½   teaspoon dill
½   teaspoon sweet
    paprika
1   to 2 tablespoons
    lemon juice
1   tablespoon honey
    Salt and pepper

STUFFING:

¾   pound bulk pork
    sausage
2   large cloves garlic,
    mashed
½   teaspoon dill
½   teaspoon sweet
    paprika

2   cups cooked Brown
    Rice (page 102)
1   egg, lightly beaten
    Salt and pepper

To prepare cabbage: Leave cabbage whole, but cut out core and carefully remove at least 12 to 14 good-sized leaves without tearing. Steam these in double boiler or steamer until soft enough to bend.

To prepare sauce: In a heavy pot, sauté onion in oil until soft. Add tomatoes, water, bouillon cube, seasonings, lemon juice, and honey to taste. Simmer, covered, while preparing the stuffing. Salt and pepper to taste.

To prepare stuffing: Brown sausage over medium heat; add garlic while browning; and then drain off any excess grease. Mix with seasonings, rice, and egg, and salt and pepper to taste. In each cabbage leaf, put 2 tablespoons of stuffing and roll tightly but gently. Place rolls in simmering sauce and slice remaining cabbage to lay on top. Simmer, covered, for at least 30 minutes. Serve in bowls with sauce. Serves 4 to 6.

    ❢Hint: Buy round steak rather than cube steak
    and ask the butcher to cube it. Round steak is
    usually cheaper than cube steak.❡

SAUSAGE-STUFFED RED PEPPERS
Approximate cost: $3.25
Protein grams: 90
Preparation time: 50 minutes

This is good during the times when peppers are on special. Serve with steamed seasonal greens and sliced tomatoes.

4	red peppers, halved lengthwise and seeded	½	teaspoon dried basil
¾	pound bulk pork sausage	½	teaspoon dried oregano
1	small onion, finely chopped	3	cups cooked brown rice
2	cloves garlic, minced	2	eggs, lightly beaten
			Salt and pepper
		1½	cups tomato juice
		½	cup grated Romano cheese

Steam peppers in double boiler or steamer for 6 to 8 minutes to soften. Brown sausage, onion, and garlic in heavy frying pan over medium heat. Drain off any excess oil. Combine meat with herbs, rice, and egg. Salt and pepper to taste. Spoon into pepper shells, and place in a shallow casserole dish or baking pan. Pour tomato juice around peppers and cover. Bake for 20 minutes in a 350-degree oven. Uncover, baste with tomato juice, and sprinkle cheese over top. Reduce heat to 300 degrees. Bake 10 minutes more. Serves 4 to 6.

LENTIL & SAUSAGE SOUP
Approximate cost: $1.80
Protein grams: 130
Preparation time: 2 hours

Serve with hot French bread or muffins and a fruit salad.

2	cups dried lentils	¾	pound bulk pork sausage
2	quarts vegetable stock or water	½	teaspoon dried oregano
1	medium onion, finely chopped	½	teaspoon dried basil
2	celery ribs, chopped	2	to 3 tablespoons tomato paste

2	**tablespoons fresh, minced parsley**	1½	**teaspoons salt**
3	**cloves garlic, mashed**	3	**tablespoons red wine vinegar**

Rinse lentils. Bring water or stock to a boil. Add lentils, and reduce heat to simmer. Cover and cook for about 40 minutes, or until lentils are tender. Add onion, celery, parsley, and garlic; continue to simmer. Brown sausage with oregano and basil, and pour off excess fat. Add meat and tomato paste to soup. Salt to taste. Simmer, covered, for another 50 minutes to an hour, and add vinegar the last 15 minutes. Serves 4 to 6.

LIVER & ONIONS

Approximate cost: $3.50
Protein grams: 50
Preparation time: 20 minutes

Serve with Oven-Fried Potatoes (page 104) and a vegetable salad.

6	**tablespoons oil**	½	**teaspoon dried rosemary**
2	**large onions, thinly sliced**	1	**cup raw wheat germ**
1	**pound calves' liver**		**Salt and pepper**
½	**teaspoon dried thyme**		

Heat 3 tablespoons oil, and sauté onions over low heat for 12 to 15 minutes until golden brown. Stir frequently. Meanwhile, trim sinew from liver, and cut into serving pieces. Mix thyme, rosemary, and wheat germ in a shallow dish. When onions have cooked, remove from pan and add remaining oil to pan. Dip liver in wheat germ and herbs, and brown lightly on both sides. Do not overcook—liver tastes better when it is a little pink. Serve covered with onions. Salt and pepper before serving. Serves 4 to 6.

❶Hint: Liver is also a powerful source of vitamin A and most of the B vitamins.❷

LIVER & ONIONS IN GRAVY
Approximate cost: $1.80
Protein grams: 28
Preparation time: 1½ hours

This is a very easy-to-prepare and a remarkably delicious dish that someone fixed for me years ago. It is another good one for the dubious liver-lover. Serve over mashed potatoes, with steamed string beans and a carrot salad.

1	pound beef liver	**Salt and pepper**
2	large onions, chopped	1½ **cups water**
1	large bay leaf	3 **to 4 tablespoons flour**
½	teaspoon dried thyme	

Trim heavy sinew from liver and cut into bite-sized pieces. Put liver and onions into a shallow casserole dish with bay leaf, and sprinkle thyme over top. Salt and pepper lightly. Pour in water, and sprinkle flour over all. Mix together and bake, uncovered, in a 350-degree oven for at least 1 hour, until onions become tender and gravy thickens. Check once or twice, and add more water, if needed, or cover lightly with foil if water cooks down too much. Serves 5 to 6.

LIVER & SAUSAGE LOAF
Approximate cost: $2.75
Protein grams: 75
Preparation time: 1 hour, 20 minutes

This was my mother's way to get us to eat liver. It is really very tasty, and the leftovers make a good sandwich filling. Serve with baked potatoes, steamed vegetables, and sliced tomatoes.

1	pound beef liver	1	teaspoon lemon juice
1	medium onion		
½	pound bulk pork sausage	1	teaspoon salt Pepper
1	cup dry bread crumbs	2	eggs, beaten
		2	strips bacon

Trim heavy sinew from liver and cover with hot water in a saucepan. Simmer for 5 minutes and drain, reserving ½ cup broth. Put liver and onion through a meat grinder or in a food processor. With a large fork, mix ground liver, onion, reserved broth, sausage, bread crumbs, lemon juice, salt, pepper, and eggs. Shape into a loaf, and cover with bacon. Bake in 325-degree oven for 1 hour. Serves 5 to 6.

POULTRY DISHES

Poultry is a major protein source in the Americas. Although its cost has risen along with that of meat, it is still a good buy, particularly when stretched with other ingredients. Buying a whole chicken and cutting it up yourself is also more economical than buying parts unless a store is running a special. A whole turkey, while often a good buy, is a large bird for a small family to consume without getting tired of it, but turkey parts, especially drumsticks and thighs, are frequently on special. They are good buys for casserole-type dishes.

A new product available in many parts of this country is ground turkey, a lean mixture that does well in casseroles, loafs, and meatballs. It is considerably cheaper than ground meat and a good protein buy. It is low fat and bland, so other ingredients added to moisten and season it are important to its preparation.

POULTRY DISHES

There are many theories on cooking poultry, and in recent years a number of special clay pot dishes and recipes designed for high heat cooking of poultry have become popular. These are useful and fun, and they are excellent for keeping the meat moist. In general, poultry is flavorful and moist when cooked at low temperature for a longer length of time.

MARINATED BAKED CHICKEN

Approximate cost (with marinades): $2.45 to $2.80
Protein grams: 160 to 195
Preparation time: 1½ to 1¾ hours

Serve a baked chicken with brown rice or bulgar wheat unless it is stuffed. Nearly any vegetable goes with chicken, and it is nice to follow the entrée with a tossed green salad.

2½ to 3-pound fryer   **Salt and pepper**
Marinade chosen
from those that
follow

To prepare chicken: Wipe chicken inside and out with a damp paper towel, then follow the directions for using one of the basting mixtures below. Preheat the oven to 450 degrees and reduce heat to 350 degrees when the bird is put in. Baste chicken with drippings or more marinade every 15 minutes during cooking. Chicken is done when leg joint moves easily. 1 to 1½ hours are required. Serves 4 to 6.

LEMON-THYME MARINADE:

2   cloves garlic,   **2   tablespoons oil**
**   mashed or grated**   **1½ teaspoons dried**
¼   cup lemon juice   **   rosemary**

Rub chicken with garlic, and place breast side down in a roasting pan. Mix together lemon juice and oil, and pour ½ of mixture over chicken. Sprinkle chicken with ½ of rosemary, and place in oven. Baste with drippings. After ½ hour, turn chicken breast side up. Pour remaining marinade over chicken, and sprinkle with remaining rosemary. Continue to baste, and salt and pepper lightly before serving.

CURRY-APPLE MARINADE:

2   cloves garlic,   **2   tablespoons oil**
**   mashed or grated**   **1½ teaspoons curry**
3   tablespoons frozen   **   powder**
**   apple juice**
**   concentrate,**
**   thawed**

Place chicken breast side down in a roasting pan. Mix together garlic, apple juice concentrate, oil, and curry. Spread ½ of mixture over chicken, and place in oven. Baste with drippings.

After ½ hour, turn bird breast side up. Pour remaining marinade over top. Continue to baste, and salt and pepper lightly before serving.

VERMOUTH-THYME MARINADE:

½ cup dry vermouth	1½ teaspoons dried
2 tablespoons oil	thyme
3 tablespoons minced onion	

Place chicken breast side down in a roasting pan. Mix together vermouth, oil, and onion, and pour ½ of mixture over chicken. Sprinkle ½ of thyme over top and place in oven. Baste with drippings. After ½ hour, turn bird breast side up. Pour remaining marinade over chicken, and sprinkle remaining thyme over top. Continue to baste, and salt and pepper lightly before serving.

ORANGE-CUMIN MARINADE:

Juice of one orange	2 tablespoons oil
1 teaspoon cumin	½ teaspoon garlic powder

Place chicken breast side down in a roasting pan. Mix together orange juice, cumin, oil, and garlic powder. Pour ½ of mixture over chicken, and place in the oven. Baste with drippings. After ½ hour, turn bird breast side up. Pour remaining marinade over top. Continue to baste, and salt and pepper lightly before serving.

CHICKEN IN MUSTARD MARINADE

Approximate cost: $3.35 to $3.65
Protein grams: 160 to 195
Preparation time (not including marinating time): 1 hour, 45 minutes

Serve with rice, steamed summer squash, and a cabbage and cucumber salad.

2½ to 3 pound fryer, cut into pieces	1½ teaspoons curry powder
½ cup honey	3 cloves garlic, grated
½ cup Dijon mustard	
¼ cup soy sauce	

46

Place chicken pieces skin-side-down in a shallow baking dish. Mix together honey, mustard, soy sauce, curry powder, and garlic, and pour over chicken. Refrigerate for 6 hours, turning chicken pieces after 3 hours. Remove chicken from marinade, and put in a covered casserole dish. Bake in a 325-degree oven for 1½ hours, and baste frequently with marinade. Uncover last half hour. Serves 4 to 6.

●Hint: A chicken 3 pounds or under is best for frying, baking, or broiling, and a large fat hen— one over 3 pounds—is best for stewing in water.●

BAKED CHICKEN WITH BULGUR-GIBLET STUFFING

Approximate cost: $3
Protein grams: 250
Preparation time: 2 hours

Serve with corn on the cob and steamed carrots.

3	pound whole fryer with giblets	2¼	cups cooked bulgur wheat
	Water	¼	teaspoon poultry seasoning
2	tablespoons oil		
¼	cup finely chopped onion	½	teaspoon dried thyme
¼	cup finely chopped celery		Salt and pepper
			Sweet paprika

Wipe chicken inside and out with a damp paper towel. Set aside. Put giblets, including neck, in a small pan and cover with water. Simmer, covered, for 10 minutes. Meanwhile, heat oil in a small frying pan, and sauté onions and celery until softened. Mix with bulgur wheat, poultry seasoning, and thyme. Remove giblets from broth, reserving broth, and discard neck. Trim gizzard and chop fine with heart and liver. Add to bulgur mixture. Salt and pepper to taste. Add 2 to 3 tablespoons broth to moisten stuffing. (Freeze remaining broth for another use.) Stuff chicken with bulgur mixture. Do not pack tightly, or stuffing will get mushy. Place chicken breast side up in a roasting pan. If bird is small, pack the extra stuffing around the opening of the cavity and cover with foil. Brush chicken generously with oil, and sprinkle with paprika. Bake in a preheated 350-degree oven for 1½ hours. Serves 5 to 6.

OVEN-FRIED CHICKEN

*Approximate cost: Nut-Crumb—$3.75; Parmesan-Wheat-Germ—
$3.90*
Protein grams: Nut-Crumb—220; Parmesan-Wheat-Germ—250
Preparation time: 1 hour, 10 minutes

Oven-Fried Chicken is nice with potato salad and a raw
vegetable plate. Recipes for two coatings follow. Both of the
following recipes for oven-fried chicken coatings can be stored
in the refrigerator and used as needed.

1	2½-pound fryer, disjointed	¾	cup buttermilk
		1	cup coating mix

To prepare chicken: Wipe dry chicken pieces and dip each
piece of chicken in buttermilk, then in coating mix. Bake on a
cookie sheet in a 325-degree oven for 1 hour, or until meat near
the bone is no longer pink. Serves 4 to 6.

NUT-CRUMB COATING:

1	cup almonds	2	teaspoons dried thyme
1½	cups dry, whole-wheat bread crumbs	1	teaspoon onion powder
½	cup toasted wheat germ	1	teaspoon garlic powder
2	teaspoons crushed, dried rosemary	2	teaspoons salt
		½	teaspoon pepper

Grind almonds fine in blender, and mix well with all other
ingredients. Store, covered, in the refrigerator. Makes about 3¼
cups.

PARMESAN & WHEAT GERM COATING:

1½	cups grated Parmesan cheese	1	teaspoon garlic powder
1½	cups raw wheat germ	1	teaspoon onion powder
1½	teaspoons salt	1	teaspoon dried thyme
½	teaspoon pepper		

Mix all ingredients well, and store, covered, in the refrigerator.
Makes slightly over 3 cups.

SORT-OF GREEK CHICKEN
Approximate cost: $2.60 to $3
Protein grams: 165 to 200
Preparation time: 1 hour, 45 minutes

A version of this recipe was given to me by a friend years ago. It's so odd and simple, and yet so tasty that everyone is surprised. Serve with Brown Rice (page 102) or pasta and vegetable salad.

1 **2½- to 3-pound fryer, disjointed**	1 **can (15-ounce) tomato sauce**
2 **tablespoons olive oil**	2 **teaspoons cinnamon**
Salt and pepper	2 **cloves garlic, grated**

Brown chicken pieces in oil in a frying pan. Salt and pepper lightly, and transfer to a shallow casserole dish. Mix together tomato sauce, cinnamon, and garlic, and pour over chicken. Cover and bake in a 325-degree oven for 1 to 1½ hours, or until chicken is very tender. Serves 4 to 6.

❡Hint: If you are not going to use the neck and back of a chicken in a dish, simmer them in water to make broth. Strain off bones and freeze broth for later use.❡

CHICKEN & BROCCOLI CASSEROLE

Approximate cost: $3.25
Protein grams: 190
Preparation time: 1 hour

This and the next recipe are made from one chicken. Buy one fresh whole chicken and disjoint. Freeze breast for the second recipe, Chicken Stir Fry. Serve with a tomato salad.

1   fresh whole chicken
3   tablespoons oil
2   large carrots, coarsely chopped
½   large onion, finely chopped
2   cups coarsely chopped fresh or frozen broccoli
2   cloves garlic, mashed

½   teaspoon dried basil
½   teaspoon dried thyme
5   cups cooked noodles or spaghetti-type pasta
    Salt and pepper
1½   cups grated Swiss cheese

Put chicken parts in a pot and add water. Simmer, covered, until chicken is tender (20 to 25 minutes). Remove chicken pieces and retain broth. Remove chicken from bones and shred. Heat oil in frying pan and sauté carrots, onion, and broccoli until slightly tender (about 8 to 10 minutes). Add garlic, basil, and thyme to vegetables, and stir in chicken and pasta. Add enough broth to moisten, and salt and pepper lightly. Transfer to a casserole dish, and top with cheese. Bake in a 350-degree oven for 15 to 20 minutes, or until all ingredients are hot and the cheese has melted. Serves 4 to 6.

CHICKEN STIR FRY

Approximate cost: $3.75
Protein grams: 125
Preparation time (not including marinating time): 35 minutes

Serve with Brown Rice (page 102) and perhaps followed by a tomato and cucumber salad.

1   chicken breast (approximately 1¼ pounds)
½   cup soy sauce
2   tablespoons white wine or vinegar
3   large cloves garlic, grated or mashed
1-   to 2-inch piece fresh ginger, grated
3   tablespoons oil
1   large carrot, diagonally and thinly sliced
¼   pound fresh string beans, diagonally sliced

1   small green pepper, seeded, halved and cut in strips
2   cups green onions, diagonally sliced
2   stalks celery, diagonally sliced
¼   pound mushrooms, sliced (optional)
2   medium zucchini, diagonally sliced
    Salt and pepper
1   to 2 dried red chili peppers, crushed (optional)
1   tablespoon cornstarch

Skin and bone chicken breast, and cut into ½-inch pieces. Mix together soy sauce, vinegar or wine, garlic, and ginger. In a bowl, combine with chicken to marinate. Refrigerate for about 3 hours, then remove chicken from marinade with a slotted spoon, retaining marinade. In a wok or large frying pan, heat oil and cook chicken for 2 to 3 minutes over a high heat. Remove chicken from pan, and add vegetables in the order listed. Cook each 2 to 3 minutes over a high heat, adding more oil, if needed. Return chicken and marinade to the pan. Salt and pepper lightly, and add 1 or 2 crushed dried chili peppers, if desired. Cover the pan, lower the heat, and steam for a few minutes—until all vegetables are tender, but still crunchy. Mix 1 tablespoon cornstarch into a little cold water. Remove cover and add the cornstarch mixture to pan juices to thicken. Stir to coat all ingredients. Serve immediately. Serves 5 to 6.

CHICKEN & LIMA BEAN STEW
Approximate cost: $4.20
Protein grams: 150
Preparation time: 50 minutes

Fix this when your store runs a special on chicken parts. Serve with a green salad. If you live in an area where cilantro (Chinese parsley) is available, it makes a delicious garnish for this dish.

6	chicken thighs or legs	½	teaspoon dried thyme
3	tablespoons oil Salt and pepper	3	cups sliced carrots
1	large onion, coarsely chopped	½	cup chicken broth
2	cloves garlic, grated	1	large package (1¼-pound) frozen lima beans (or canned equivalent known as butter beans)
1	can (1-pound) canned tomatoes		Chopped fresh cilantro
½	teaspoon dried basil		

In a heavy soup pot or Dutch oven, brown chicken pieces in oil. Salt and pepper lightly, and remove from pan with a slotted spoon. Add onion and garlic, and sauté in drippings until soft. Return chicken to pot, and add tomatoes, herbs, carrots, and chicken broth. Simmer, covered, for 20 minutes. Add beans, and continue to simmer for 10 to 15 minutes more. Salt and pepper to taste. Garnish with cilantro, if desired. Serves 4 to 6.

SUMMER CHICKEN STEW
Approximate cost: $3.90 to $4.20
Protein grams: 200 to 235
Preparation time: 1 to 1½ hours

Serve with raw carrot and celery sticks or a tossed green salad.

3 tablespoons oil	1 teaspoon dried basil
1 2½- to 3-pound broiler/fryer, cut into pieces	1 teaspoon dried oregano
Salt and pepper	½ teaspoon dried thyme
1 red onion, halved and sliced	½ cup chicken broth
3 cloves garlic, grated	5 cups hot, cooked noodles
1 small green pepper, seeded and cut into strips lengthwise	2 tablespoons cornstarch
1 small eggplant, peeled and chopped	⅓ cup grated Parmesan cheese
2 large tomatoes, diced	3 tablespoons fresh, minced parsley

Heat oil in heavy frying pan. Brown chicken well over a medium heat. Salt and pepper lightly, and transfer to a casserole. Sauté onion and garlic in remaining oil until softened. Add green pepper, eggplant, tomatoes, seasonings, and broth. Salt lightly and heat to boiling. Pour over chicken. Cover casserole and bake in a 350-degree oven for 50 to 60 minutes, or until chicken is tender and vegetables are saucy.

Spread noodles on a serving platter, and arrange chicken and vegetables on top. Reheat remaining liquid. Mix cornstarch with a little cold water, and stir into liquid to thicken. Pour over chicken, and top with cheese and parsley. Serve immediately. Serves 5 to 6.

❻Hint: When preparing chicken salad for sandwiches, purée the cooked skin with a little broth or water, and add it to the mixture for more flavor.❾

GINGER & GARLIC CHICKEN
Approximate cost: $2.50 to $3
Protein grams: 160 to 195
Preparation time (not including marinating time): 1 hour, 10 minutes

Serve with Brown Rice (page 102), sautéed zucchini, and a tomato salad.

⅔	cup soy sauce	2½	tablespoons minced ginger
¼	cup dry white wine	2½	to 3 pound fryer, disjointed
2	tablespoons honey		
3	garlic cloves, mashed or grated		

Combine soy sauce, wine, honey, garlic, and ginger in a jar with a lid. Shake well to mix. Put chicken pieces in a shallow baking dish or casserole, and pour marinade over chicken. Let sit in the refrigerator for 4 to 5 hours, turning pieces periodically. Bake, uncovered, in a 350-degree preheated oven for about 1 hour, or until chicken is tender. Turn frequently during cooking. Serves 4 to 6.

⬤Hint: Uncooked chicken has a short lifetime. Keep it tightly covered in the refrigerator, and use it within a day or two of purchase.⬤

TURKEY TOSTADAS
Approximate cost: $3.20
Protein grams: 15
Preparation time: 1 hour, 15 minutes

This is a popular Mexican-American dish. Serve alone or with refried beans.

3	turkey drumsticks, weighing about ¾ pound each	2	cups grated mild white cheese
3½	cups finely shredded cabbage	3	to 4 tablespoons oil
3	tablespoons lemon juice	4	to 5 corn tortillas Hot pepper sauce (optional) Sour cream Avocados, sliced (optional)
2	large tomatoes, chopped		
1	medium onion, finely chopped		

Steam drumsticks in a steamer or above water for about 1 hour, or until done. (Steaming keeps the meat moist.) Cool, skin, and remove meat from bones; chop or shred it. (While drumsticks are cooking, shred cabbage and toss with lemon juice and refrigerate. Prepare tomatoes, onion, and cheese and refrigerate.) When turkey meat is ready, heat some oil in a frying pan, and fry tortillas lightly on both sides. Top tortillas with turkey and a dash of hot pepper sauce. Salt lightly and sprinkle with cheese. Place tortillas under the broiler to melt cheese. Remove and top with onions, tomatoes, and cabbage. Add a dollop of sour cream and sliced avocado. Serve immediately. Serves 4 to 5.

Note: Leftover cooked turkey or chicken can be used in tostadas, too.

❧Hint: A frozen turkey should defrost in the refrigerator so it stays juicy.❧

❧GROUND TURKEY DISHES❧

This recipe and the two that follow are made with uncooked ground turkey that is found in many supermarkets today. It tends to be very lean and requires oil and/or moisture in cooking.

TURKEY LOAF
Approximate cost: $1.75
Protein grams: 160
Preparation time: 1 hour, 15 minutes

Serve with baked potatoes, corn on the cob, and string beans.

1 small onion, finely chopped	Dash hot pepper sauce
1 medium carrot, finely grated	3 pieces fresh bread, crumbled
2 tablespoons fresh, minced parsley	½ teaspoon poultry seasoning
¼ cup oil	1 teaspoon salt
1 egg, lightly beaten	Pepper
3 tablespoons catsup	1 pound raw ground turkey
⅓ cup chicken or turkey broth	

Sauté onion, carrot, and parsley in oil until softened. Meanwhile, mix together egg, catsup, turkey or chicken broth, hot pepper sauce, and crumbled bread. In a mixing bowl, combine vegetables, bread mixture, poultry seasoning, salt, a dash of pepper, and turkey. Stir with a large fork until well mixed. Shape into a loaf, and set in a shallow baking dish or loaf pan and bake in a 350-degree oven for 1 hour. Serves 4 to 6.

Note: This mixture can be used to make turkey burgers, too. Fry in a little oil and serve between Whole-Wheat Buns (page 86) or covered with a cheese sauce.

TURKEY LASAGNA

Approximate cost: $2.85
Protein grams: 200
Preparation time: 1 hour

Serve with a tossed green salad and raw carrot sticks.

½ medium onion, finely chopped	8 to 10 cooked lasagna noodles
3 cloves garlic, minced or grated	1½ cups cottage cheese or ricotta cheese
4 tablespoons oil	1 egg, lightly beaten
1 pound raw ground turkey	1 package (10-ounce) frozen spinach, steamed
1 teaspoon salt	
1 teaspoon oregano	
1 teaspoon dried basil	1½ cups grated mozzarella cheese
1 can (15-ounce) tomato sauce	

Sauté onion and garlic in oil until softened. Add turkey and brown lightly. Stir in salt, and set mixture aside. Mix seasonings with tomato sauce, and set aside. Beat cottage cheese or ricotta cheese with egg. Lay 4 to 5 cooked lasagna noodles the length of a 7½-by-11½-inch baking pan. Spread turkey mixture over this, and top with half of the sauce. Over this, spread the cottage cheese mixture and the spinach. Cover with remaining lasagna noodles, and pour remainder of sauce over top. Top with grated cheese and cover with foil. Bake in a 350-degree oven for about 25 minutes. Serves 5 to 6.

TURKEY & RICE MEATBALLS
Approximate cost: $1.90
Protein grams: 160
Preparation time: 45 minutes

Serve with a green vegetable and a carrot-and-cabbage salad.

1 small onion, finely chopped	1 egg, lightly beaten
½ cup finely chopped green pepper	1 teaspoon salt
3 cloves garlic, mashed	½ teaspoon dried thyme
¼ cup oil	½ teaspoon poultry seasoning
1 pound raw ground turkey	3 tablespoons oil
1½ cups cooked Brown Rice (page 102)	1 cup turkey or chicken broth

Sauté onion, pepper, and garlic in ¼ cup oil until softened. Transfer to a mixing bowl with turkey, rice, egg, and seasonings. Stir with a large fork until well mixed, and form into small balls. Heat oil in heavy-bottom pan and brown turkey balls carefully. Add broth and simmer, covered, for 20 minutes. Serves 4 to 6.

❧LEFTOVER TURKEY DISHES❧

The next three recipes are for leftover turkey. They are particularly useful for those times when you have cooked a large holiday bird. Actually, buying a 10- or 12-pound turkey on special is a good idea if you take the time to put the leftovers in freezer bags for later. It is easy to get tired of turkey if you fix the leftovers four days in a row.

TURKEY HASH
Approximate cost: $3.25
Protein grams: 180 to 190
Preparation time: 35 minutes

Serve with coleslaw and sliced tomatoes.

1	medium onion, finely chopped	2	cups stuffing
2	medium carrots, coarsely grated	½	cup turkey gravy
		½	cup milk
¼	cup oil		Salt, pepper, and sage
3	cups cooked, chopped turkey	4	to 6 poached eggs

Sauté onion and carrots in oil until softened. Add turkey and stuffing, and heat through, stirring frequently. Add gravy and milk, and season to taste. Turn heat down to simmer. Make a well for each egg. Crack in eggs, cover and cook until eggs are just set. Serves 4 to 6.

TURKEY & HERBED EGGS IN POCKET BREAD

Approximate cost (with bread): $2.35
Protein grams (with bread): 180
Preparation time: 25 to 30 minutes

Serve with a spinach salad and sliced tomatoes.

⅓	cup finely chopped green onion	6	eggs, lightly beaten
⅓	cup finely chopped green pepper	1	teaspoon dill
			Salt and pepper
3	tablespoons oil	4	to 6 warm pocket breads (also called Pita Bread)
2	cups cooked, finely chopped or shredded turkey		

Sauté onions and pepper in oil in a frying pan until softened. Stir in turkey, and heat through. Add eggs and dill, and stir and cook until set. Salt and pepper to taste. Stuff in pita breads. Serves 4 to 6.

●Hint: It is cheaper to buy a whole chicken and disjoint it yourself. Use a sharp knife and kitchen scissors. It's also cheaper to bone chicken breasts yourself.●

TURKEY CHOWDER

Approximate cost: $3
Protein grams: 150
Preparation time: 40 minutes

Serve with a carrot and cucumber salad and Corn Muffins (page 88).

1 large onion, chopped	1 can (1-pound) tomatoes
3 tablespoons butter or margarine	2 medium potatoes, peeled and coarsely grated
3 cups cooked turkey, shredded or chopped	Salt and pepper
1 can (10¾- ounce) turkey broth (or homemade equivalent)	1 package (10-ounce) frozen corn Nutmeg
1 cup water	1 can (5.33-ounce) evaporated milk

In a soup pot, sauté onion in butter or margarine until softened. Stir in turkey, broth, water, tomatoes, and potatoes. Salt and pepper lightly and cover pot. Simmer for 20 minutes, breaking up tomatoes. Stir in corn, and add nutmeg and more salt and pepper to taste. Stir in milk just before serving. Serves 4 to 6.

MARINATED TURKEY THIGHS

Approximate cost: $3.75 to $4.25
Protein grams: 400 to 460
Preparation time (not including marinating time): 1½ hours

A nice dish for company, and tastes somewhat like roast lamb. Serve with Bulgur Wheat (page 103), julienned carrots, and a tossed green salad.

3 to 4 turkey thighs, weighing about 3½ to 4 pounds	2 tablespoons olive oil
2 cups dry red wine	4 to 5 garlic cloves, slivered
	Fresh or dried rosemary

Skin and bone thighs by slitting meat on either side of the bone and lifting the bone out as you cut under it. Lay boned thighs in a shallow baking dish, and pour over wine. Brush with oil, and cover with garlic slivers and rosemary to taste. Cover with foil, and marinate in the refrigerator for 5 to 6 hours, turning 2 or 3 times. Bake in a 350-degree, preheated oven for about 1 hour, or until done. Baste frequently, during cooking. Serves 5 to 6.

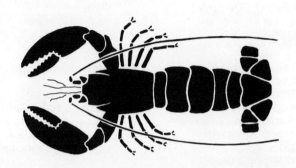

SEAFOOD
DISHES

Seafood is an excellent source of protein. In fact, it is superior to meat in protein quality because it is easier for the body to utilize. Two of the cheaper seafood buys, cod and squid, are practically pure protein and contain almost no fat. You do not need to consume great quantities of seafood to add adequate protein to your diet.

Unfortunately, seafood, like meat, has risen in price in recent years, and unless you live near lakes, streams, or have access to fresh coastal fish, you are better off economically using canned seafood. (Even living by the ocean as I do, seafood prices are generally high unless some particular fish is in season and abundant.) Although some frozen fish fillets and squid are often reasonably priced, and work especially well when extended in casseroles and chowders, the best buys are generally canned tuna, oysters, clams, and salmon. However, clams and salmon have risen in price and you may want to stock up during sales. Canned seafood, primarily tuna, is the main ingredient of the recipes in this section. When fixed in multi-ingredient recipes, tuna is quite delicious, and it is certainly versatile. All canned seafood keeps indefinitely, and it can be used to make good last-minute protein-rich meals.

QUICK FRIED FISH

Approximate cost: $4.50 to $5
Protein grams: 220
Preparation time: 25 minutes

Serve with tartar sauce (if desired), a baked potato, and a carrot and cabbage salad.

FISH:

- **¾ cup corn meal**
- **⅓ cup raw wheat germ**
- **⅓ cup grated Parmesan cheese**
- **1 teaspoon garlic powder**
- **1 teaspoon onion powder**
- **1 teaspoon dried thyme**
- **1 teaspoon salt**
- **6 frozen fish fillets (cod, snapper, flounder, turbot)**
- **4 to 6 tablespoons oil**

TARTAR SAUCE:

- **¼ cup mayonnaise**
- **¼ cup unflavored yogurt**
- **2 tablespoons minced onion**
- **2 tablespoons pickle relish**
- **2 teaspoons prepared horseradish**

To prepare fish: Mix together corn meal, wheat germ, cheese, and seasonings. Spread on a plate. Rub frozen (not thawed) fillets each with a tablespoon of oil, and then coat with corn meal mixture. Place close together but not touching in an oiled baking pan or broiler pan. Place fish under a medium broiler for 10 to 12 minutes, or until fish flake easily. Serves 4 to 6.

To prepare tartar sauce: Mix together all ingredients. Serve with fish.

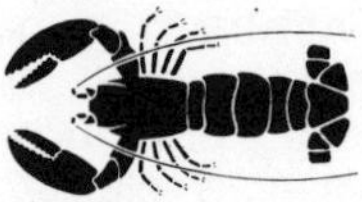

Hint: As a rule, do not turn fish fillets when broiling them. The heat of the pan is sufficient to cook both sides.

SESAME COD
Approximate cost: $5
Protein grams: 200
Preparation time: 20 minutes

Serve with Brown Rice (page 102), mixed vegetables, and sliced tomatoes.

1 **egg**	½ **cup flour**
4 **tablespoons evaporated milk**	4 **to 5 tablespoons oil**
	Salt and pepper
½ **cup bread crumbs**	**Fresh, chopped**
½ **cup sesame seeds**	**parsley**
6 **cod fillets**	**Lemon wedges**

Beat egg and milk together. Mix bread crumbs and sesame seeds, and spread on a plate. Dip fillets in egg and milk mixture, then dust with flour, and coat with crumbs and sesame seeds. Heat oil in a large frying pan, and fry fish over a medium heat on both sides until it flakes easily. Salt and pepper lightly, garnish with parsley, and serve with lemon wedges. Serve 4 to 6.

●Hint: Do not overcook fish. It is ready when it loses its translucency.●

SALMON LOAF
Approximate cost: $3.75
Protein grams: 125
Preparation time: 1 hour

Canned salmon—especially pink salmon—is no longer the bargain it once was, but it is available sometimes on a great special. That is the time to pull out the following recipes, although these are computed at regular prices. This is a variation of my Aunt Margaret Hull's Salmon Loaf. Serve with baked potatoes, a steamed green vegetable such as broccoli, and sliced tomatoes.

1 **can (15½-ounce) pink salmon**	3 **tablespoons lemon juice**
¼ **cup margarine**	½ **teaspoon salt**
¼ **cup low-fat milk**	**Dash of pepper**
2 **eggs, separated**	**Lemon wedges**
¼ **cup minced onion**	

Drain liquid from canned salmon, and reserve. In a saucepan combine margarine, milk, and salmon liquid. Heat until margarine melts. Meanwhile, flake salmon in a bowl, and combine with egg yolks, onion, lemon juice, salt, and pepper. Stir in liquid mixture and beat well. Beat egg whites until stiff, fold into salmon mixture, and turn into a well-oiled·9-by-5-by-3-inch loaf pan. Bake in a preheated 350-degree oven for 35 to 40 minutes, or until puffed and set. Serve with lemon wedges (or for kids, with tartar sauce). Serves 4 to 6.

●Hint: When poaching a fish in court bouillon, add a little lemon juice and milk to preserve the whiteness of the fish.●

SALMON QUICHE
Approximate cost: $3.90
Protein grams: 120
Preparation time: 1 hour

This is a nice company supper, especially if served with a light green salad or artichokes and small bowls of vegetable soup.

1 **can (7¾-ounce) salmon**	2 **tablespoons grated Parmesan or Romano cheese**
½ **cup minced green onion**	1 **9-inch single unbaked pie shell (page 96)**
4 **tablespoons butter or margarine**	
2 **tablespoons fresh, minced parsley**	3 **eggs**
½ **cup grated Swiss cheese**	1¼ **cups light cream (half-and-half)**
	½ **teaspoon salt**
	Lemon wedges

Drain salmon and flake, reserving liquid. Sauté onion in butter or margarine until softened, and add parsley. Distribute salmon, onion, parsley, and cheese in the pie shell. Beat eggs with cream, reserved salmon liquid, and salt. Pour over salmon mixture, and put filled pie shell into a preheated 450-degree oven for 8 minutes. Reduce heat to 375 degrees, and bake for about 25 to 30 minutes, or until filling is set. Serve with lemon wedges. Serves 6.

SALMON & ZUCCHINI SPAGHETTI

Approximate cost: $4.20
Protein grams: 125
Preparation time: 40 minutes

Serve with spinach salad and French bread.

⅓ cup olive oil	½ teaspoon dried basil
½ small onion, chopped	½ teaspoon dried oregano
2 garlic cloves, minced	⅛ teaspoon cayenne pepper
4 cups fresh, peeled, chopped tomatoes	1½ cups chopped zucchini
2 tablespoons fresh chopped parsley	Salt
1 can (15½-ounce) red salmon, drained and flaked	¾ pound spaghetti Grated Romano cheese

Heat oil in a large frying pan or skillet, and sauté onions and garlic over medium heat until onions are softened and garlic is golden. Stir in tomatoes, parsley, salmon, oregano, basil, and cayenne pepper. Bring to a boil, and simmer, uncovered, for about 10 minutes. Add zucchini and simmer for another 4 to 5 minutes. Salt to taste. Meanwhile, cook spaghetti and drain. Mix hot pasta with sauce and sprinkle with grated cheese. Serves 5 to 6.

●Hint: To remove fish odor and grease from the cooking pan, boil ½ cup vinegar in the pan before washing it. To remove fish odor from your hands, rub them with salt before you wash them.●

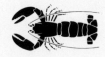

❧SQUID DISHES☙

Squid is one of the great economies of the Western world. Although it is not available fresh in many areas, it can often be found in the frozen fish section in 2- to 3-pound packages. Because it is pure protein, it freezes beautifully.

To clean squid, wash well, and remove head from body right below the eyes. Cut the tentacles from head, and save. Discard the head. Pull soft white intestines and firm spine from inside the body tube, and discard, along with thin white membrane and fins from the outside of the body. The remainder—the body tube and tentacles—is what you cook, although in many parts of the world, every part but the spine is eaten.

SQUID MARINARA

Approximate cost (not including pasta): $3.25
Protein grams (not including pasta); 220
Preparation time (after cleaning squid): 50 to 60 minutes

Serve over pasta accompanied by a spinach salad.

½	medium onion, thinly sliced	½	teaspoon dried oregano
2	cloves garlic, mashed	½	teaspoon dried thyme
4	tablespoons olive oil	2	tablespoons red wine vinegar
⅓	cup fresh, minced parsley	1½	cups water
4	cups peeled and chopped tomatoes		Pinch of saffron (optional)
½	teaspoon dried basil		Salt and pepper
		2	pounds cleaned squid

Sauté onion and garlic lightly in oil. Add parsley, tomatoes, herbs, vinegar, water, and saffron. Cover and simmer for 35 to 40 minutes, or until well blended. Salt and pepper to taste. When sauce is thoroughly heated, cut squid bodies into rings and add to sauce along with tentacles. Cook only until bodies turn white. Squid cooks very fast, and overcooking makes it tough. Remove from heat, and serve immediately over pasta. Serves 5 to 6.

ZUCCHINI-STUFFED SQUID

Approximate cost: $3.40
Protein grams: 215
Preparation time (after cleaning squid): 45 minutes

Serve with Brown Rice (page 102) or Pilaf (page 102) and a tossed green salad.

2 pounds squid, cleaned (approximately 12 bodies)	3 cups grated zucchini
1 small onion, finely chopped	½ cup ricotta or cottage cheese
2 cloves garlic, mashed	Salt
¼ cup fresh, minced parsley	½ cup dry white wine (vermouth is also good)
1 teaspoon dried basil	Chopped fresh parsley

Mince squid tentacles, and leave bodies whole for stuffing. Sauté onion, garlic, and parsley until softened. Add tentacles, and sauté until color changes. Stir in basil. Press out liquid and stir zucchini into mixture. Sauté for 2 to 3 minutes. Remove from heat, and stir in cheese and salt to taste. Cool slightly, and stuff squid bodies rather loosely. Lay stuffed squid close together in a shallow baking pan, and pour wine over top. The water in the squid will cook out and add to the liquid. Cover and place in a 350-degree preheated oven for 12 to 14 minutes, or until squid turns white. Transfer to a serving platter, and spoon a little cooking juice over top. Garnish with parsley. Serves 4 to 5.

DEVILED TUNA

Approximate cost (including rice or with toast): $3.50
Protein grams (including rice or with toast): 170
Preparation time: 20 to 25 minutes

Serve with steamed greens and sliced tomatoes.

3 tablespoons butter or margarine

3 tablespoons flour

2½ cups warm milk

¼ cup powdered milk

¼ teaspoon dry mustard

1 package (10-ounce) frozen peas

1 can (12½-ounce) tuna, drained and flaked

3 hard-boiled eggs, chopped

Dash of pepper sauce

Salt and pepper

Cooked Brown Rice (page 102) or whole-wheat toast

Hot or sweet paprika

Lemon wedges

Melt butter or margarine in large saucepan. Stir in flour to make a golden roux. Mix milk and powdered milk, and add slowly. Stir until sauce begins to thicken. Then stir in mustard, peas, tuna, and chopped eggs. Season to taste. Serve over rice or toast, garnished with paprika and lemon wedges. Serves 4 to 6.

TUNA & VEGETABLE CASSEROLE

Approximate cost: $3
Protein grams: 120
Preparation time: 25 minutes

Serve with a tomato salad and raw carrot sticks.

3 cups uncooked egg noodles

2 quarts water

1 small onion, minced

2 tablespoons oil

¼ cup fresh, minced parsley

2 cups shredded cabbage

1 teaspoon dried dill

1 can (7½-ounce) tuna, drained and flaked

1 package (10-ounce) frozen peas

Salt and pepper

1½ cups grated cheddar cheese

Bring water to a boil, and add noodles. Reduce heat. Meanwhile, in a large frying pan with a lid, sauté onion in oil until well softened. Stir in parsley, cabbage, and dill, and continue to cook, stirring frequently, until cabbage is limp. Stir in tuna, peas, and noodles, and heat through. Salt and pepper to taste. Over this sprinkle a little water, and then sprinkle with cheese. Cover and cook over low heat until cheese is melted. (Do not let mixture get dry.) Serves 5 to 6.

TUNA & VEGETABLE CHOWDER

Approximate cost: $3
Protein grams: 90
Preparation time: 35 to 40 minutes

Serve with Corn Muffins (page 88) and a tossed green salad.

2	large potatoes, peeled and diced	½	teaspoon dried oregano
2	large carrots, diced	½	teaspoon dried basil
1½	quarts water	1	large can (12½-ounce) tuna, drained and flaked
2	bottles (8-ounce) clam juice		
2	strips bacon, diced	1	cup peas, fresh or frozen
1	medium onion, minced	2	cups diced zucchini Salt and pepper
1	small green pepper, minced	1	can (5.33-ounce) evaporated milk Lemon wedges
¼	cup fresh, minced parsley		
½	teaspoon dried thyme		

Put potatoes and carrots in a soup pot with water and clam juice. Bring to a boil, reduce heat and simmer, covered, for 10 minutes. Meanwhile, in frying pan, cook bacon until almost crisp. Then add onion, pepper, and parsley and sauté until softened. Add to soup pot, along with tuna and herbs. Simmer, covered, for 8 to 10 more minutes, then add peas and zucchini and salt and pepper to taste. Simmer about 5 minutes more; remove from heat; and add milk just before serving. Serves 5 to 6.

❝Hint: If you serve a whole fish, save the bones and carcass for making a fish stock to use in soups or for poaching fish.❞

❧CLAM SAUCES FOR PASTA❧

Clam sauces are delicious served over spaghetti or green noodles along with raw carrot sticks and a tossed green salad. (Canned clams are often on special.)

RED SAUCE

Approximate cost (including pasta): $5
Protein grams (including pasta): 80
Preparation time: 1 hour

3	tablespoons olive oil	1	can (6-ounce) tomato paste
1	small onion, minced	1	cup water
2	cloves garlic, minced	2	bottles (8-ounce) clam juice
1	cup minced celery	2	cans (6½-ounce) minced clams, with
½	teaspoon dried basil		liquid reserved
½	teaspoon dried oregano		Salt
¼	teaspoon dried thyme	6	cups cooked spaghetti or linguini
1	can (1-pound) tomatoes		Grated Romano cheese
			Minced parsley

Heat oil in a large frying pan, and sauté onion, garlic, and celery until softened. Stir in seasonings, tomatoes, tomato paste, and water. Bring to a boil, reduce heat, and simmer, uncovered, until well blended and thickened (about 30 minutes). Add clam juice, and continue to simmer for another 20 minutes. Add clams. Salt to taste. Serve over hot pasta garnished with cheese and parsley. Serves 4 to 6.

❺Hint: Pan-fry or sauté lean fish; bake fatty fish such as mackerel and tuna.❻

WHITE SAUCE

Approximate cost (including pasta): $4.20
Protein grams (including pasta): 75
Preparation time: 30 minutes

Serve over spaghetti accompanied by a green salad and sliced tomatoes.

4	tablespoons butter or margarine	2½	tablespoons flour
2	cloves garlic, minced	2	bottles (8-ounce) clam juice
3	tablespoons fresh, minced parsley	2	cans (6½-ounce) minced clams
1	teaspoon dried basil	¼	cup dry white wine
			Salt and pepper
		6	cups cooked spaghetti

Heat butter or margarine in a large frying pan, and sauté garlic and parsley until softened. Stir in basil and flour, and cook, stirring over low heat for 5 minutes. Add clam juice slowly and cook until thickened. Stir in clams and white wine. Salt and pepper to taste. Serve over hot pasta. Serves 4 to 5.

❧CLAM CHOWDERS❧

Here are the traditional clam chowders served in North America—"red" and "white" as they are often called.

MANHATTAN STYLE
Approximate cost: $4.25
Protein grams: 45
Preparation time: 45 minutes

Serve with Corn Muffins (page 88) and a tossed green salad.

2	strips bacon, diced	½	teaspoon dried oregano
1	large onion, diced		
1	cup minced celery	½	teaspoon thyme
2	large potatoes, peeled and diced	2	cans (6½-ounce) minced clams, with liquid reserved
1	can (1-pound, 12-ounce) tomatoes		Salt and pepper
2	cups clam juice		Grated Romano cheese
1	teaspoon dried tarragon		

In a heavy-bottomed soup pot or Dutch oven, fry bacon over a medium heat until slightly crisp. Lower heat, and add onion and celery. Sauté in bacon fat until softened. Add potatoes, tomatoes, clam juice, seasonings, and clams. Break tomatoes. Cover pot and simmer for 30 minutes, then salt and pepper to taste. Serve with grated Romano cheese. Serves 5 to 6.

BOSTON STYLE
Approximate cost: $4
Protein grams: 45
Preparation time: 45 minutes

Serve with coleslaw and Soy and Wheat-Sesame Bread (page 85).

Follow directions for Manhattan Style Clam Chowder, but substitute 1 quart water for tomatoes, and omit oregano. Simmer 15 minutes, then add 1 13-ounce can evaporated milk. Serve immediately and without cheese. Serves 5 to 6.

Note: For variety, add canned or frozen sweet corn to this recipe.

OYSTER STEW
Approximate cost: $3.20
Protein grams: 100
Preparation time: 25 minutes

Serve with grilled cheese sandwiches and a green salad.

1 tablespoon butter or margarine	2 cups peeled and diced potatoes
2 tablespoons oil	1 cup water
1 cup chopped celery with leaves	1½ quarts whole milk
½ cup green onions	Salt and pepper
2 cans (8-ounce) oysters, with liquid reserved	Cayenne pepper

Heat butter or margarine and oil in a heavy-bottomed soup pot. Sauté celery and onions until softened. Drain oysters, reserving liquid. Chop into small pieces, and add to vegetables. Cook until edges curl. Add potatoes, reserved oyster liquid, and water, and bring to a boil. Reduce heat, cover, and simmer for 10 to 12 minutes, or until potatoes are tender. Stir in milk slowly. Heat through, and season to taste. Serves 4 to 6.

❥Hint: Fresh fish does not keep well. Plan to cook it the day you buy it or at the latest, the day after. Wrap it tightly in foil or plastic for the refrigerator so the odor will not dominate.❥

SALADS
&
DRESSINGS

This section draws on the recipes of the previous chapters, containing recipes for entrée salads using meat, fish, poultry, and vegetarian protein. Again, observe the suggested accompaniments to the vegetarian salads for protein balance.

Entrée salads have become very popular in recent years and the advent of the salad bar in restaurants has been a pleasant answer to the needs of those with lighter appetites. Certainly a salad supper is welcome in the heat of the summer—especially if you have had a substantial lunch.

Salad entrées are economical because they do well at stretching the protein ingredients. Of course, it's important to use seasonal vegetables for economy, but it is easy to vary ingredients in a salad and still come out with a winner. And salads can often be made with leftovers. At the end of this section are several dressing recipes. Although each recipe calls for a specific dressing, feel free to vary them to your taste.

71

MOROCCAN VEGETABLE SALAD

Approximate cost: $2.90
Protein grams: 45
Preparation time (without chilling time): 25 minutes

Serve with Soy and Wheat-Sesame Muffins (page 89) and fresh fruit.

½ **pound mushrooms, whole**	1 **cup unflavored yogurt**
2 **green peppers, coarsely chopped**	½ **cup Mayonnaise (page 81)**
2 **red peppers, coarsely chopped**	2 **cloves garlic, mashed**
1 **dozen cherry tomatoes, halved**	2 **tablespoons olive oil**
¾ **cup chopped scallions**	1 **tablespoon lemon juice**
1 **can (3¼-ounce) pitted black olives, halved**	1 **teaspoon cumin**
1 **can (15-ounce) garbanzo beans (chick peas), drained**	⅛ **teaspoon turmeric**
	Salt and pepper
	Spinach leaves or any seasonal green

Steam mushrooms until slightly softened. Cool and mix with peppers, tomatoes, scallions, olives, and beans and chill a couple of hours. Mix together yogurt, mayonnaise, garlic, olive oil, lemon juice, cumin, and turmeric. Toss salad with dressing just before serving, and salt and pepper to taste. Arrange on plates on beds of spinach leaves. Serves 4 to 6.

●Hint: Add leftover salad to vegetable soup the next day. With the dressing, it adds a nice tang.●

BROWN RICE & NUT-SEED SALAD

Approximate cost (including dressing): $1.50
Protein grams: 65
Preparation time: 20 to 25 minutes

Serve with Zucchini Muffins (page 90) and fresh fruit.

4 cups cooked Brown Rice (page 102)	**⅔ cup shelled sunflower seeds**
1½ cups diced celery	**Curry Vinaigrette**
1½ cups shredded cabbage	**Dressing (page 80)**
½ cup finely chopped green onions	**Salt and pepper**
⅔ cup salted peanuts	**Sliced tomatoes**
	Sliced cucumbers

Combine rice, celery, cabbage, green onions, peanuts, and seeds. Chill well. Dress with Curry Vinaigrette Dressing, and salt and pepper to taste. Arrange on plates on bed of sliced tomatoes and cucumbers. Serves 4 to 6.

●Hint: Grating root vegetables into a salad is a good way to get children to eat vegetables.●

SHRIMP & BROWN RICE SALAD

Approximate cost (including dressing): $3
Protein grams: 50
Preparation time: 20 to 30 minutes

Serve with Soy and Wheat-Sesame Muffins (page 89) and fresh fruit.

5 cups cooked Brown Rice (page 102)	**⅓ pound cooked, fresh, tiny shrimp**
1 cup cooked peas	**Salt and pepper**
1 cup finely chopped red onion	**Mustard Vinaigrette**
½ cup finely chopped green pepper	**Dressing (page 80)**
½ cup fresh, minced parsley	**Spinach leaves**
	Sliced tomatoes

Combine rice, peas, onion, pepper, parsley, and shrimp. Chill well, then toss with Mustard Vinaigrette Dressing, and salt and pepper to taste. Arrange on plates on spinach leaves surrounded by 3 or 4 slices of tomatoes. Serves 4 to 6.

TABOULI WITH CHICKEN

Approximate cost: $2.75
Protein grams: 60
Preparation time (without soaking and chilling time): 15 minutes

Tabouli is a classic Middle Eastern salad. Adding chicken makes the dish a more nutritious and filling entrée salad. Serve with Soy and Wheat-Sesame Muffins (page 89) and with stewed fruit.

2 cups raw bulgur wheat	⅓ cup chopped fresh mint (or 2½ tablespoons dried)
2 cups cold water	
1 cup fresh, minced parsley	½ cup olive oil
1 cup green onion	½ cup lemon juice
2 medium tomatoes, peeled and chopped	Salt
	Romaine lettuce leaves
1 to 1½ cups chopped, cooked chicken	Sliced cucumbers
	3 tomatoes, cut into wedges

Rinse bulgur wheat in cold water, then combine with the 2 cups cold water and let stand for about 1 hour, until swelled and softened. Drain well. Combine bulgur with parsley, onion, chopped tomatoes, chicken, and mint. Toss with oil and lemon juice, and salt to taste. Cover and chill until serving (at least 1 hour). Arrange lettuce leaves and sliced cucumbers on a serving plate. Heap tabouli in a mound on top and surround with tomato wedges. Serves 4 to 6.

❡Hint: Try lightly steaming vegetables such as beans, peas, broccoli, cauliflower, or mushrooms before adding them to a salad.❡

SALMON & VEGETABLE SALAD

Approximate cost: $3.00
Protein grams: 75
Preparation time (without chilling time): 25 minutes

Serve with Corn Muffins (page 88) and fresh fruit.

1 **can (15½-ounce) pink salmon**	½ **cup finely chopped green onion**
1 **cup fresh or thawed frozen peas**	**Dill Vinaigrette Dressing (page 80)**
1 **cup diced celery**	**Salt and pepper**
2 **cups shredded cabbage**	**Sliced tomatoes**
	3 **hard-cooked eggs**

Drain and flake salmon. Discard any skin. Mix with peas, celery, cabbage, and onion. Chill for 2 to 3 hours. Just before serving, toss with Dill Vinaigrette Dressing, and salt and pepper to taste. Arrange on plates on beds of sliced tomatoes, and garnish with sliced hard-cooked eggs. Serves 4 to 6.

TUNA & WALNUT-STUFFED TOMATOES

Approximate cost: $3.40
Protein grams: 120
Preparation time: 25 minutes

This is a good summer supper salad. Serve with Zucchini Muffins (page 90) and sliced melon.

1 **can (15½-ounce) tuna, drained and flaked**	3 **tablespoons buttermilk**
1½ **cups diced celery**	1 **teaspoon lemon or lime juice**
½ **cup minced onion**	½ **teaspoon curry powder**
1 **cup chopped walnuts**	**Salt and pepper**
½ **cup Homemade Mayonnaise (page 81)**	4 **to 6 ripe tomatoes**
	Lettuce leaves

Combine tuna, celery, onion, and walnuts. Thin mayonnaise with a little buttermilk, and add to tuna mixture to taste. Add a little lemon or lime juice, curry powder, salt, and pepper to taste.

Core tomatoes, and cut from the top in six sections to ½ inch above the bottom so tomatoes flower out. Spoon tuna salad on tomatoes, and serve on lettuce leaves. Serves 4 to 6.

●Hint: Buttermilk is a good thinning agent for salad dressings made with mayonnaise, sour cream, or cottage cheese—it adds zest.●

EGGPLANT & TUNA SALAD

Approximate cost: $3.50
Protein grams: 85
Preparation time (not including drying and chilling time):
20 minutes

Serve with Zucchini Muffins (page 90) and fresh fruit.

1	large eggplant Salt	1	cup sliced green olives
6	tablespoons olive oil	1	can (6½-ounce) tuna, drained and flaked
3	cloves garlic, mashed	1⅓	cups unflavored yogurt
1	medium onion, sliced	½	cup mayonnaise
2	ribs celery, chopped	1	teaspoon dried oregano
10	cherry tomatoes, halved	1	teaspoon dried basil
6	Italian pickled peppers		Salt and pepper Lettuce leaves
½	cup shelled sunflower seeds		Lemon wedges

Chop eggplant coarsely, but do not peel. Salt lightly, and let sit in a colander for one hour to drain. Sauté half the eggplant with half the mashed garlic in 3 tablespoons oil about 6 to 8 minutes, until softened and darkened. Repeat with remaining eggplant, garlic, and oil. Remove from pan with slotted spoon, and mix with onion, celery, tomatoes, peppers, sunflower seeds, olives, and tuna. Chill mixture for about 2 hours. Mix together yogurt, mayonnaise, oregano, and basil. Toss with salad mixture just before serving. Salt and pepper to taste. Arrange on plates on beds of lettuce leaves. Garnish with lemon wedges. Serves 4 to 6.

ITALIAN SQUID SALAD
Approximate cost: $3.20
Protein grams: 280
Preparation time (after cleaning squid and
after marinating time): 25 to 30 minutes

Serve with raw carrot sticks, hot French bread, and cheese.

2	**pounds squid**	½	**cup mayonnaise**
¼	**cup olive oil**	2	**tablespoons white**
1½	**tablespoons fresh**		**wine vinegar**
	lemon juice	2	**teaspoons anchovy**
	Dash of pepper		**paste**
	Dash of celery salt		**Romaine lettuce**
2	**cups chopped**		**leaves**
	celery	3	**hard-boiled eggs**
3	**green onions, finely**	3	**large tomatoes**
	chopped		

Clean squid (see page 64). Bring 2 quarts of water to boil, and drop squid in water. Cook several minutes—just long enough for squid to lose its translucency and turn white. (Overcooking toughens squid.) Remove from water, drain, and chill. Mix together olive oil, lemon juice, pepper, and celery salt. Dice squid, toss with mixture, and marinate for several hours. Just before serving, mix with celery and onions. Then combine mayonnaise, vinegar, and anchovy paste, and add to squid mixture. Salt to taste. Arrange lettuce leaves and top with squid salad on a serving platter. Surround with quartered eggs and tomatoes. Serves 5 to 6.

●Hint: Remove fresh fish from the refrigerator about 20 minutes before you cook it to improve flavor. Frozen fish should be thawed in the refrigerator to retain the juices. It should be cooked immediately after it is thawed.●

❧THE SALAD BAR❧

Many restaurants are offering the salad bar option as a response to our new calorie-, health-, and budget-consciousness. I find this a nice at-home entertainment choice, too, especially in the summer or for a lunch party. The following recipes and amounts are adequate to serve a group of twelve, but you can adjust the quantities for any size group.

I suggest offering a choice of dressings. Basic Vinaigrette, Dilled Buttermilk Dressing, and Green Goddess Dressing go well with this salad. Accompany by hot bread and butter and chilled fruit juice or wine.

Approximate cost (including recipes and all suggestions): $20
Protein grams (including recipes and all suggestions): 650
Preparation time (including recipes and all suggestions):
1½ to 2 hours

BASIC SALAD BOWL

2 **heads romaine lettuce**	1 **large bunch spinach**
2 **heads butter lettuce** OR	3 **large carrots, grated**
1 **large head iceberg lettuce**	

Wash and dry lettuce and spinach, and tear into salad-size pieces. Toss in a large salad bowl with grated carrots. Dress *very lightly* with Basic Vinaigrette, if desired. Serves 12.

BEAN & PEPPER BOWL

1 **can (15-ounce) kidney beans**	1 **large green pepper, quartered and thinly sliced**
1 **can (15-ounce) garbanzo beans**	2 **tablespoons lemon juice**

Drain beans, and rinse with clear water. Drain well, and toss in a serving bowl with green pepper and lemon juice.

POTATO & OLIVE BOWL

2	pounds red-skinned potatoes	1	handful chopped fresh cilantro (Chinese parsley) or regular parsley
1	can (2¼-ounce) sliced black olives	3	tablespoons cider vinegar

Wash potatoes well, and cook in skins. When tender, drain and cool. Slice and toss with olives and cilantro or parsley, and sprinkle with vinegar. Chill slightly.

In addition, a salad bar should include some of the following; each served in a separate bowl.

½	small head red cabbage, finely shredded	6	hard-boiled eggs, grated
4	bunches scallions, chopped	⅓	pound fresh or canned shrimp
1	pound cherry tomatoes, halved	3	cans (6½-ounce) water-packed tuna
4	cups alfalfa sprouts	1½	cups sunflower seeds
1	pound Swiss cheese, coarsely grated		

BASIC VINAIGRETTE DRESSING

Approximate cost: $.35
Protein grams: negligible
Preparation time: 5 minutes

This dressing is delicious on greens, mixed vegetables, and rice and pasta salads. It is even nice over a winter fruit salad. Some variations follow the basic recipe.

½	cup oil (mixture olive and safflower, sesame, or sunflower oils)	½	teaspoon brown sugar
¼	cup white wine vinegar	½	teaspoon Dijon mustard
2	cloves garlic, minced	½	teaspoon dried thyme
		½	teaspoon salt
		⅛	teaspoon pepper

Mix all ingredients, and shake well.

CURRY VINAIGRETTE:

Substitute for thyme: 1 teaspoon curry powder and ¼ teaspoon
each coriander and cumin
Then add: 1 tablespoon mayonnaise

DILL VINAIGRETTE:

Add: 1 teaspoon dill

ITALIAN VINAIGRETTE:

Substitute red wine vinegar for white wine vinegar
Add: 1 tablespoon mayonnaise
¼ teaspoon each dried oregano and basil

MUSTARD VINAIGRETTE:

Add: 1 teaspoon Dijon mustard
1 tablespoon mayonnaise

Note: If you prefer making vinaigrette dressing on the salad, then dribble the oil over first. It will coat the leaves so that the vinegar and herbs will cling to them.

●Hint: Any vinaigrette dressing makes a good
marinade for meat, fish, or chicken.❥

HOMEMADE MAYONNAISE
Approximate cost: $.70
Protein grams: 12
Preparation time: 5 minutes

This makes a wonderful dip for cold, raw vegetables, and for steamed chilled vegetables such as artichokes, broccoli, and asparagus. Chopped fresh herbs, minced parsley, or cilantro can be added to vary the mayonnaise.

2 **egg yolks**	½ **teaspoon Dijon**
2 **tablespoons white**	**mustard**
wine vinegar	**Dash salt**
2 **tablespoons lemon**	1 **cup oil (I use**
juice	**safflower.)**

In a blender put egg yolks, vinegar, lemon juice, mustard, and salt. Blend until smooth. Then switch blender to lowest speed and slowly but steadily add oil until mixture thickens. Then add the rest of the oil more quickly. (It may be necessary to stop the blender and stir once the mixture thickens before resuming the blending.) Store, covered, in the refrigerator. Makes 1½ cups.

GREEN GODDESS DRESSING
Approximate cost: $.70
Protein grams: negligible
Preparation time: 5 minutes

This is a great dressing for chunky (rather than leafy) salads. It also makes a good dip for raw or steamed chilled vegetables, and I like it with seafood salads.

1½ **cups Mayonnaise**	1 **teaspoon anchovy**
(above)	**paste**
⅓ **cup fresh, minced**	2 **cloves garlic,**
parsley	**mashed**
⅓ **cup fresh, minced**	1 **tablespoon lemon**
watercress	**juice**
1 **teaspoon crushed,**	**Salt to taste**
dried tarragon	

Mix all ingredients well. Store, covered, in the refrigerator. Makes about 2 cups.

DILLED BUTTERMILK DRESSING

Approximate cost: $.70
Protein grams: 17
Preparation time: 5 minutes

½ cup buttermilk
½ cup low-fat cottage
    cheese
1 teaspoon onion
    powder

½ teaspoon garlic
    powder
1 teaspoon dill
    Salt and pepper

Put buttermilk and cottage cheese in blender, and blend smooth. Blend in seasonings. Salt and pepper to taste. Store in the refrigerator. Makes 1 cup.

YOGURT OLIVE DRESSING

Approximate cost: $.70
Protein grams: 11
Preparation time: 6 to 8 minutes

This dressing reminds me of an incredibly rich sandwich spread I ate in college. It was made of mayonnaise, cream cheese, and chopped olives—on sourdough French bread. I can't eat that combination in good conscience now, but this dressing is far less caloric and very good on greens or a hearty vegetable salad.

1 cup unflavored
    yogurt
½ cup Mayonnaise
    (page 81)
3 tablespoons
    chopped olives

Dash of hot pepper
sauce
Salt and pepper to
taste

Mix all ingredients well. Makes about 1⅔ cups.

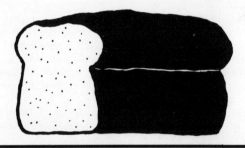

BREADS

These recipes should augment those in the rest of the book and help to create an overall balance of protein at a meal. All the recipes are easy to prepare, and the muffin recipes are especially quick. The emphasis is on healthful ingredients to prevent your eating empty calories: after all, breads are all fairly high in calorie content, so we might as well make them body-building as well.

In general, these bread recipes are economical, although the concentration is on the quality of ingredients more than economy (for the above reasons). Yeast breads do take time, a commodity that is precious to everyone, but a good cook can always find other things to do while a yeast bread is rising, and there is no more satisfying form of kitchen creativity than freshly baked bread.

OATMEAL BREAD

Approximate cost: $1.20
Protein grams (two loaves): 80
Preparation time (not including refrigeration): 2½ hours

This is an easy bread containing plenty of yeast and eggs. It does not have to be kneaded, just refrigerated.

2 **packages dry yeast**	1 **teaspoon salt**
½ **cup lukewarm water**	4 **cups unbleached flour**
1½ **cups boiling water**	2 **eggs, beaten**
1 **cup quick oats**	1 **cup whole-wheat flour**
½ **cup molasses**	
⅓ **cup oil**	

Soften yeast in lukewarm water for 10 minutes. Combine boiling water, oats, molasses, oil, and salt. Cool to lukewarm, and stir in 2 cups of unbleached flour, softened yeast, and the eggs. Stir in remaining flour to make sticky dough. Transfer to well-oiled bowl and cover. Refrigerate for at least 2 hours, or overnight. Turn out dough on well-floured surface, and shape into 2 loaves. Place in oiled bread pans. Set, covered, in a warm place until the dough is doubled in bulk. Bake in preheated, 350-degree oven for about 50 minutes, or until browned. Cool slightly before removing loaves from pans. Makes 2 loaves.

●Hint: Use hard-wheat flour for yeast breads whenever possible. This is the wheat that is harvested in the Midwest in the spring.●

RELIABLE RYE BREAD

Approximate cost: $1.20
Protein grams (2 loaves): 120 to 130
Preparation time: 2 hours, 50 minutes

This recipe came from my mother's family—fine cooks all of them. It's not a heavy rye, as you can tell by the ingredients, but it's a lovely one.

2	packages dry yeast	2	cups dark rye flour
½	cup warm water	2	tablespoons anise
2	cups milk or water		seed
⅓	cup molasses	1	tablespoon salt
⅓	cup brown sugar	5	to 6 cups
2	tablespoons oil		unbleached flour

Dissolve yeast in warm water. Meanwhile, heat milk or water with molasses, sugar, and oil, just enough to blend. The mixture must only be lukewarm, or it will kill the yeast. Add yeast, rye flour, anise seed, and salt. Beat well with hand or electric mixer. Mix in unbleached flour, 1 cup at a time. Turn out onto floured surface, and knead for 6 to 8 minutes or until smooth and elastic. Put dough into well-oiled bowl, and turn to coat all of dough. Cover, and let rise in a warm place until double in bulk. Punch down, divide, shape into 2 loaves, and place in oiled bread pans. (The dough can be shaped into round loaves or rolls.) Let rise 40 minutes. Bake in preheated, 350-degree oven for 35 to 40 minutes or until nicely browned. Cool before removing from pan.

❡Hint: For a smoother texture and a browner crust, use milk in dough. For a less cakelike quality and a crisper crust, use water in dough.❡

SOY & WHEAT-SESAME BREAD

Approximate cost (2 loaves): $1.60
Protein grams (2 loaves): 250
Preparation time: 4 hours

This is a hearty, healthful bread that makes good sandwiches and toast. Slice it thin when serving it for dinner.

2	packages dry yeast	1	egg
⅓	cup lukewarm water	⅓	cup oil
⅓	cup molasses	1	tablespoon salt
2	cups water	1	cup soy flour
1	cup gluten flour	⅓	sesame seeds
5½	cups whole-wheat flour		

BREADS

In a large mixing bowl, dilute yeast in lukewarm water and stir in molasses. Let mixture sit 5 minutes, then add water, gluten flour, and 2 cups whole-wheat flour. Beat with an electric or hand mixer for 4 to 5 minutes. Cover with damp cloth and set in a warm place until doubled in bulk (about 1 hour). Stir down flour mixture. In a small bowl beat egg with oil and salt and add to batter with soy flour, sesame seeds, and remaining whole-wheat flour (retaining ½ cup for kneading). Mix well (dough will be sticky) and turn out on floured board. Knead for 8 to 10 minutes, working in flour for kneading. (Oil hands, if necessary, rather than adding more flour which makes the bread heavy.) Shape dough into a ball. Put in a well oiled bowl and let rise, covered, until doubled in bulk. Punch down, knead again briefly, and shape into 2 loaves. Place in greased 9-by-5-by-3-inch bread pans and let rise for 20 to 25 minutes. Bake in a preheated 400-degree oven for 10 minutes, then reduce heat to 350 degrees. Bake for about 40 minutes more, or until golden brown. Makes 2 loaves.

Note: Gluten flour is found in natural or health food stores.

WHOLE-WHEAT HAMBURGER BUNS

Approximate cost: $.80
Protein grams: 85
Preparation time: 2 hours, 40 minutes

1 package dry yeast	2⅓ cups whole-wheat flour
1½ cups warm water	
½ cup milk	2 cups unbleached flour
¼ cup (½ stick) margarine, melted	
2 tablespoons honey	2 unbeaten egg whites
2 tablespoons molasses	4 tablespoons sesame seeds
1 teaspoon salt	

Soften yeast in ¼ cup lukewarm water in large mixing bowl. Beat in remaining water, milk, margarine, honey, molasses, and salt. Reserve ⅓ cup flour for kneading. Add remaining flour, 1 cup at a time, using electric beater until dough is too stiff for beaters, then mix, using a spoon. Turn out on floured board, and knead several minutes. Place in oiled bowl, and turn dough in bowl to coat entire surface. Cover with damp cloth, and let rise in a warm area until double in bulk. Lightly grease 2 baking sheets. Punch down dough. With a rolling pin, roll out dough on floured board to ¼-inch thickness. Cut into 24 3½-inch rounds, using scraps if necessary. Place on baking sheets, and let rise for 1 hour in a warm place. Brush 12 rounds with egg white, and sprinkle 1 teaspoon sesame seeds on top of each. Place in preheated, 375-degree oven for 12 to 14 minutes. Place sesame seed tops on 12 buns. Makes 1 dozen double buns.

●Hint: Too much salt slows the rising action of the yeast.●

BRAN MUFFINS

Approximate cost: $1.25
Protein grams (total): 80
Preparation time: 30 minutes

This is an easy recipe because you can make the batter in advance, put it in the refrigerator, and spoon into however many muffin cups you want at a time. The batter keeps for at least 2 weeks.

1 cup flaked bran (not commercial cereal)	2 cups buttermilk
1 cup boiling water	2 cups All-Bran cereal
½ cup margarine, slightly softened	2½ cups unbleached flour
½ cup brown sugar or honey	2½ teaspoons baking soda
2 eggs	1 teaspoon salt

Combine flaked bran and boiling water. Meanwhile, cream margarine with sugar or honey. Add eggs, buttermilk, and All-Bran cereal. Into this mixture sift flour, baking soda, and salt. Combine with bran-flakes mixture, and stir until well blended. Store, covered, in refrigerator until needed. Fill greased muffin cups to within ⅔ of top. Bake in preheated, 375-degree oven for 20 minutes. Makes 28 to 30 muffins.

BROWN-RICE MUFFINS

Approximate cost: $.40
Protein grams: 50
Preparation time: 30 minutes

This is a good way to use leftover Brown Rice (page 102).

1 cup whole-wheat flour	2 tablespoons brown sugar (optional)
½ cup unbleached flour	2 eggs
3 teaspoons baking powder	¾ cup milk
1 teaspoon salt	¼ cup melted margarine or oil
	¾ cup cooked Brown Rice

Mix together flours, baking powder, salt, and sugar. In a separate bowl, beat eggs with milk and margarine or oil. Combine with dry ingredients, add rice, and stir only until all ingredients are moistened. Spoon into greased muffin cups, and bake in preheated, 400-degree oven for 18 to 20 minutes, or until golden brown. Cool slightly. Makes 12 muffins.

❥Hint: To enhance their taste, serve muffins warm rather than piping hot.❥

CORN MUFFINS

Approximate cost: $.55
Protein grams: 48
Preparation time: 40 minutes

1 cup yellow corn meal	½ teaspoon baking soda
1 cup sour milk or buttermilk	1 teaspoon baking powder
½ cup unbleached flour	1 scant teaspoon salt
½ cup whole-wheat flour	3 tablespoons brown sugar (optional)
	2 eggs
	¼ cup oil

Soak corn meal in sour milk or buttermilk for 10 minutes. Meanwhile, mix together flours, baking soda, baking powder, salt, and sugar. Beat eggs with oil, and add to dry mixture. Stir in corn meal mixture, blending only until ingredients are moistened. Spoon into lightly greased muffin cups, and bake in preheated, 375-degree oven for about 20 minutes, or until golden brown. Cool slightly. Makes 12 muffins.

❡Hint: Once dry ingredients have been combined with the liquid in a quick bread recipe, be, careful not to overstir.❡

SOY & WHEAT-SESAME MUFFINS

Approximate cost: $.65
Protein grams: 60
Preparation time: 35 minutes

These are highly nutritional muffins made of complementary proteins. They are a good accompaniment for vegetarian dishes.

1¼	cups whole-wheat flour	
¼	cup soy flour	
3	tablespoons sesame seeds	
3	tablespoons brown sugar (optional)	
3	teaspoons baking powder	
½	teaspoon salt	
1	egg, separated	
¾	cup milk	
¼	cup oil	

Mix together flours, sesame seeds, sugar, baking powder, and salt. Beat egg yolk with milk, then stir in oil. Add liquid ingredients to dry ones, and stir only enough to moisten all ingredients. Beat egg white stiff and fold into batter. Spoon into greased muffin cups, and bake in preheated, 400-degree oven for 20 minutes, or until golden brown. Makes 12 muffins.

❡Hint: Cooled, quick breads can be frozen and then reheated (frozen) in foil.❡

ZUCCHINI MUFFINS

Approximate cost: $.50
Protein grams: 50
Preparation time: 40 minutes

Here is another way to utilize your giant zucchini crop.

1 **cup whole-wheat flour**	2 **eggs**
1 **cup unbleached flour**	5 **tablespoons oil**
3 **teaspoons baking powder**	¾ **cup milk**
¾ **teaspoon salt**	1 **cup medium grated zucchini**
1 **teaspoon cinnamon**	
3 **tablespoons brown sugar**	

Mix together flours, baking powder, salt, cinnamon, and sugar. Beat eggs with oil and milk, and stir into dry ingredients. Stir just enough to moisten all ingredients. Stir in zucchini, and spoon into greased muffin cups. Bake in preheated, 375-degree oven for about 20 minutes, or until golden brown. Makes 12 muffins.

●Hint: Use solid shortening rather than oil to grease bread pans—it makes removing the bread an easier task.●

DESSERTS

Desserts are desserts—we must face the basic fact that most of them are not essential to our nutritional needs. However, some desserts are sweeter, richer, and more caloric than others, and some are definitely more expensive.

The following recipes are a collection of ideas that do not disrupt a tight budget, and offer a variety of meal-ending tastes. I have even included the protein grams for these dishes, because in many instances they are substantial.

I regard desserts as gifts for special occasions and company, and I think that even if economy (and calories) are an issue in your household, you will probably feel the same way.

FIGS IN VANILLA CREAM

Approximate cost: $1.25
Protein grams: 7
Preparation time (not including chilling): 15 minutes

This doesn't sound like much, but it is delicious—even to me, the one who never liked figs, fresh or canned. And it couldn't be easier.

1 **jar or can (1-pound) figs**	1½ **teaspoons vanilla**
1½ **cups water**	3 **tablespoons honey**
1 **cinnamon stick, broken in halves**	½ **cup light cream (half-and-half)**

Drain figs, if canned, and rinse lightly. Put figs in a saucepan with water, cinnamon stick, vanilla, and honey. Cover and simmer for 6 to 8 minutes. Remove cinnamon sticks, and divide figs and honey liquid among 4 dessert dishes. Chill well. Just before serving, stir 2 tablespoons of cream into each dish. Serves 4.

Note: This recipe can easily be doubled.

STEWED APPLES WITH CUSTARD SAUCE

Approximate cost: $1.50
Protein grams: 28
Preparation time: 40 minutes

STEWED APPLES:

4 **cups peeled, cored, and chopped tart apples**	⅓ **cup apple juice or cider**
½ **cup raisins**	1 **teaspoon cinnamon**
	¼ **cup brown sugar, packed**

CUSTARD SAUCE:

3 **egg yolks**	**Dash salt**
2 **tablespoons honey**	2 **cups scalded milk**
1 **teaspoon vanilla**	

To prepare apples: In a saucepan combine apples, raisins, juice or cider, and cinnamon. Cover and simmer for 12 to 15 minutes, stirring occasionally. Add sugar during the last few minutes of cooking. Cool and chill. Serve in dessert dishes topped with Custard Sauce.

To prepare sauce: In a saucepan beat together egg yolks, honey, vanilla, and salt. Slowly add milk, beating with a wooden spoon. Stir and cook over low heat until mixture is thickened and coats the back of spoon. Do not boil. Serve chilled or warm over stewed apples. Serves 6.

●Hint: Rinsing a pan before scalding milk helps prevent scorching.●

MAPLE BAKED APPLES

Approximate cost (without sour cream or yogurt): $1.40
Protein grams: 25
Preparation time: 1 hour

This is a perfect dessert for a winter evening soup supper.

6	medium to large red apples (suggested: Rome Beauty)	½	cup apple juice or cider
⅔	cup chopped almonds	3	tablespoons butter or margarine
½	cup maple syrup		Nutmeg
			Sour cream or unflavored yogurt

If necessary, trim small slice from apple bases so they will stand upright. Core apples to within ½ inch of bottom, and make a shallow cut around the middle of the apples to allow for expansion during cooking. Fill centers with equal amounts of almonds, and set apples in a shallow pan without touching. Heat syrup, juice or cider, and butter or margarine in a small saucepan until mixture is well blended. Pour over and around apples. Sprinkle tops with nutmeg. Bake in a 375-degree, preheated oven for 40 minutes, basting frequently. Serve warm with sour cream or yogurt. Serves 6.

LEMON PUDDING

Approximate cost: $.60
Protein grams: 25
Preparation time: 1 hour

A childhood favorite, this is still one of my favorite desserts.

½ **cup honey**
1 **tablespoon softened butter**
3 **tablespoons unbleached flour**
⅓ **cup fresh lemon juice**

2 **teaspoons finely grated lemon peel**
2 **eggs, separated**
1 **cup milk**
⅛ **teaspoon salt**

Beat together honey and butter, and then add flour, lemon juice, and peel. Beat in yolks and milk; add salt; and stir until mixture is well blended. Beat egg whites until stiff, and fold into lemon mixture. Turn into 1-quart baking dish. Set in a pan of hot water in 325-degree oven for 40 to 45 minutes, or until set. Serve warm or cool. Serves 4 to 5.

●Hint: When measuring molasses, honey, or syrup, grease the measuring cup with butter or margarine for easy pouring.●

HONEY & NUTMEG PARFAIT

Approximate cost: $1.25
Protein grams: 35
Preparation time: 2 hours

2 **cups milk**
2 **tablespoons cornstarch**
2 **eggs, separated**
½ **cup honey**

1 **teaspoon vanilla**
¼ **teaspoon nutmeg**
1 **cup heavy cream (whipping cream)**

Blend milk and cornstarch in saucepan. Beat in egg yolks, honey, vanilla, and nutmeg. Stir over medium heat until mixture is thickened, then remove from heat. Lay waxed paper over surface so that skin will not form; cool slightly; and place in refrigerator. When mixture is chilled, beat egg whites until stiff.

Whip the cream, and fold both into pudding mixture. Spoon into 6 to 8 parfait glasses, and sprinkle with a bit of nutmeg. Set in freezer for at least 3 hours. Twenty minutes before serving, remove from freezer to soften slightly. Serves 6 to 8.

ORANGE & STRAWBERRY WHIP

Approximate cost: $2
Protein grams: 22
Preparation time (not including chilling time): 15 minutes

This is a good ending to a heavy meal—and it is fairly light in the calorie department.

2 **tablespoons (2 packages) unflavored gelatin**
⅔ **cup water**
1 **package (20-ounce) frozen strawberries (unsweetened)**

⅓ **cup honey**
   Juice of 1 orange
3 **tablespoons orange liqueur**
1 **cup unflavored yogurt**
4 **egg whites**

Soften gelatin in water over heat as directed on package. Transfer to blender, along with strawberries, honey, orange juice, and orange liqueur. Blend until smooth. Transfer to mixing bowl, and stir in yogurt. Beat egg whites until stiff, and fold into mixture. Pour into 4 to 6 dessert dishes, and chill until firm. Serves 4 to 6.

> ❝Hint: When you are cooking pudding on the top of the stove, do not stir it continually. This stops it from boiling quickly, and the bottom will then tend to scorch.❞

PINEAPPLE COCONUT SHERBET

Approximate cost: $1.65
Protein grams: 14
Preparation time (not including freezing time): 10-12 minutes

This is a light and low-calorie finish to a hearty meal.

2 cans (7½-ounce each) crushed pineapple packed in its own juice
1 pint unflavored yogurt

½ cup unsweetened, shredded coconut Toasted, slivered almonds

Combine pineapple, yogurt, and coconut, and blend well. Pour into shallow freezer tray, and freeze until mushy. Transfer to mixing bowl, and beat vigorously for 5 minutes. Return to tray and cover. Freeze until solid. Before serving, beat sherbet until smooth. Spoon into dessert dishes, and garnish with toasted almonds. Return to freezer for 20 minutes. Serves 4 to 5.

SOY AND WHEAT-SESAME PIE CRUST

Approximate cost: $.50
Protein grams: 28
Preparation time: 15 minutes

This is a delicious pie crust for entrée pies and quiches. It's especially good with a vegetarian filling, because the protein in the crust complements the vegetable protein. This crust can be used for a dessert pie, too, although you may prefer the following version for that use.

¾ cup whole-wheat pastry flour
¼ cup soy flour
¼ cup sesame seeds

½ teaspoon salt
½ teaspoon baking powder
⅓ cup cold margarine
¼ cup cold water

Stir together flours, sesame seeds, salt, and baking powder. Cut in margarine with pastry blender or knives until mixture resembles coarse meal. Add water and stir to form ball. Flour hands and board and roll out to fit a 9-inch pan. (This recipe can be doubled.) Fill and bake as directed. Makes 1 single pie shell.

●Hint: A tender, flaky pie crust depends on using cold fat with the flour and on working it in before it melts. Add ice water to help prevent the fat from melting.●

UNBLEACHED-FLOUR PIE CRUST

Approximate cost: $.25
Protein grams: 9
Preparation time: 12 to 15 minutes

You may prefer this crust for dessert pies. Try it with Custard Filling (below) or the Pear and Sour-Cream Filling (page 98).

1 cup unbleached flour	⅓ cup cold margarine
½ teaspoon salt	3 to 4 tablespoons ice water

Mix together flour and salt and cut in margarine with pastry blender or knives until mixture resembles coarse meal. Add ice water 1 tablespoon at a time and stir to form a workable ball. Flour hands and board and roll out dough to fit 9-inch pie pan. Fill and bake as directed. Makes 1 single pie shell.

CUSTARD PIE FILLING

Approximate cost (not including pie shell): $.75
Protein grams (not including pie shell): 55
Preparation time: 1 hour

4 eggs	3 cups milk
½ cup honey or brown sugar	1 9-inch, unbaked pie shell (above)
1 teaspoon vanilla	1 egg white, slightly beaten
½ teaspoon salt	
¼ teaspoon nutmeg	

Beat eggs with honey or sugar, vanilla, salt, and nutmeg. Scald milk, and beat into egg mixture slowly. Brush pie shell with egg white; let sit one minute; and then pour filling into pie shell. Bake in preheated, 425-degree oven for 15 minutes. Reduce heat to 350 degrees, and bake until center is set (until a knife comes out clean)—about 30 minutes. Serves 6.

PEAR & SOUR CREAM PIE FILLING

Approximate cost (not including pie shell): $2.20
Protein grams (not including pie shell): 20
Preparation time: 45 minutes

2	eggs	2	cans (1-pound each)
½	cup brown sugar		pear slices, drained
½	teaspoon grated		and patted dry
	lemon rind	¼	cup unbleached
¼	teaspoon nutmeg		flour
¼	teaspoon ginger	3	tablespoons brown
¼	teaspoon salt		sugar
1½	cups sour cream	¼	teaspoon nutmeg
1	9-inch, unbaked pie	3	tablespoons butter
	shell (page 97)		or margarine,
			partially hardened

Beat together eggs, sugar, lemon rind, spices, salt, and sour cream. Pour ½ of mixture into pie shell. Arrange pear slices over this; cover pears with remaining sour cream mixture. Mix together flour, sugar, and nutmeg; cut in butter or margarine to make coarse crumbs and sprinkle over pie filling. Bake in preheated, 400-degree oven for 25 to 30 minutes, or until pie is set. Cool before cutting. Serves 6.

VERY MOIST OATMEAL CAKE

Approximate cost: $1.80
Protein grams: 55
Preparation time: 1 hour

CAKE:

1¼	cups boiling water	1	teaspoon baking
1	cup quick oats		soda
½	cup margarine	1	teaspoon baking
1½	cups brown sugar		powder
2	eggs	½	teaspoon salt
1⅓	cups whole-wheat	¼	teaspoon nutmeg
	pastry flour		

TOPPING:

3 tablespoons melted butter or margarine	3 tablespoons light cream or evaporated milk
½ cup brown sugar	⅓ cup nuts
1 cup unsweetened, shredded coconut	

To prepare cake: Pour boiling water over oats, and let sit for 20 minutes. Meanwhile, cream together margarine and sugar, and beat in eggs. Combine with oatmeal. Stir together flour, baking soda, baking powder, salt, and nutmeg, and combine well with moist mixture. Pour into lightly oiled 9-by-13-inch baking pan, and bake at 350-degrees for 35 to 40 minutes.

To prepare topping: While cake is baking, mix together topping ingredients. Spoon over cake when it is done. Put under broiler for 3 minutes. Cool and serve.

BANANA NUT CAKE WITH CREAM CHEESE FROSTING

Approximate cost: $2.25
Protein grams: 70
Preparation time: 1 hour

CAKE:

¾ cup soft margarine	1 teaspoon baking soda
1 cup brown sugar, packed	1 teaspoon baking powder
2 eggs	½ teaspoon salt
1 cup mashed banana (about 2 medium)	¼ teaspoon mace
1 teaspoon vanilla	⅔ cup buttermilk or sour milk
1 cup whole-wheat pastry flour	½ cup chopped walnuts
⅔ cup unbleached flour	

FROSTING:

1 package (8-ounce) cream cheese	1 to 2 teaspoons vanilla
2 to 3 tablespoons honey	

To prepare cake: Cream margarine and sugar with an electric beater until light and smooth. Add eggs and continue to beat for 2 minutes, then add bananas and vanilla and beat for 3 to 4 more minutes. In a separate bowl, mix dry ingredients and add to banana mixture alternately with buttermilk or sour milk. Continue to beat well for several minutes, then stir in nuts. Turn into greased 8- or 9-inch round baking pans and bake in preheated 375-degree oven for 20 to 25 minutes. Cool before frosting.

To prepare frosting: Beat ingredients together, adding honey and vanilla to taste. Spread between cooled cake layers, on top, and the sides. Refrigerate until serving.

BASIC
RECIPES

Every cookbook needs a miscellaneous section—if only to gather up loose ends. Most of what you will find here are recipes and instructions for fixing ingredients or dishes that are necessary to recipes in other sections in this book. The preparation of grains is important to any modern cook who deals with vegetarian recipes. Too, many kinds of whole-grain pastas are available now, a familiarity with these will suggest many new entrée ideas. The other recipes are little touches that I hope add to the overall use of the book.

BROWN RICE

Approximate cost: $.40
Protein grams: 30
Preparation time: 45 minutes

This is the basic recipe for what is often also referred to as "steamed" brown rice (it cooks by steaming over a low heat). You can use either the short-grain or long-grain variety in this recipe.

4 cups water	**1 teaspoon salt**
2 cups brown rice	

In a saucepan bring water to a boil, and add rice. Do not stir. Sprinkle with salt. Reduce heat to simmer and cover. Cook for 30 to 40 minutes (depending on heat and altitude), or until water is absorbed and rice is tender. Makes about 5 cups.

Note: For maximum success with this recipe, use no fewer than 2 cups of rice, (although you can double that amount). Cooked rice is wonderful to have on hand to scramble with eggs in the morning or to add to soups, casseroles, and salads.

BROWN RICE PILAF

Approximate cost: $.35—.70
Protein grams (not including chicken stock, if used): 34
Preparation time: 1 hour or so

For best results use long-grain brown rice in this recipe. This is good with chicken or fish and with ethnic dishes.

3 tablespoons butter or margarine	**1 bay leaf**
½ cup finely chopped onion	**3 cups boiling water, vegetable, or chicken stock**
1 large clove garlic	**Salt**
1½ cups long-grain brown rice	

In a saucepan heat butter or margarine, and sauté onions for 2 to 3 minutes. Grate in garlic. Add rice and stir once to coat grains; turn heat to high and let the mixture get very hot; then remove from the heat. Add boiling water or stock and bay leaf. Salt lightly, especially if using chicken stock, and cover tightly. Return to heat, and simmer for 45 minutes, or until rice is tender and liquid is absorbed. (The top will have formed little craters.)

BULGUR WHEAT

Approximate cost: $.35 to $.55
Protein grams: 40
Preparation time: 20 minutes

Bulgur wheat is the wheat kernel that has been cracked and toasted to speed up the cooking time. In the supermarkets it is sold in small packages under the trade name Ala. It is good with meat, poultry, or fish, and in vegetarian dishes. It is widely used in Middle Eastern dishes. Uncooked, it can be soaked and turned into a saladlike appetizer or spread called tabouli. (See page 74.)

3 teaspoons oil	4 cups meat or
2 cups raw bulgur	vegetable stock or
wheat	water
1 teaspoon salt	

In a frying pan with a tight-fitting lid, heat oil and sauté bulgur for 4 to 5 minutes. (All grains should be coated.) Reduce heat to simmer; stir in salt; and add stock or water. Cover and cook, about 15 minutes, until all liquid is absorbed and bulgur is tender. Serves 5 to 6.

Note: Minced onions or chopped mushrooms can be added during sautéeing.

BUCKWHEAT GROATS

Approximate cost: $.45
Protein grams: 44
Preparation time: 30 minutes

Buckwheat has a very distinctive flavor. Unlike regular wheat products, it is not a cereal grain, but rather, is a herbaceous plant. Buckwheat is grown extensively in Siberia, and it is a staple in Russian cuisine. It is also referred to as Saracen wheat and Kasha. It is also a traditional component of certain Jewish dishes. I think it has a wonderful taste—not only in buckwheat pancakes, but also when fixed as an accompaniment to meat or fish.

2 cups buckwheat	1 teaspoon salt
groats	4 cups boiling water
2 eggs, slightly	
beaten	

Put groats and eggs in a heavy-bottom frying pan, and cook over high heat for 3 to 4 minutes, stirring continually so egg does not stick. After all grains are dry and separate, sprinkle salt over this, and add boiling water. Reduce heat to simmer, cover, and cook 20 to 25 minutes, until water is absorbed. Serves 5 to 6.

WHOLE-GRAIN PASTA

In the vegetarian section of this book, I have recommended using whole-grain pastas whenever possible to increase and balance the protein content of the dish. These pastas are commonly made from whole-wheat, soy and wheat, brown rice, sesame, buckwheat, artichoke, and spinach. They can be found in natural and health food stores, special sections of supermarkets, and in specialty food stores. Sometimes they are packaged like the regular commercial pastas, and their packages then carry directions for cooking. More often, though, they are sold in bulk without cooking directions. The cooking process is the same for all pastas, except that more cooking time is needed for whole-grain pastas to become tender. Fresh pastas cook more quickly than do dried ones.

To cook pasta, use a large, deep pot so the water will not boil over. Allow 4 quarts water to every pound of pasta. Salt the water, and bring it to a boil. Add the pasta and a little oil to keep it from sticking. Boil for 10 to 15 minutes, or until pasta is fork tender but not mushy. (Test on the side of the pan.) Remove the pot from the heat, and add a glass of cold water to stop the cooking process. Drain the pasta well. It is now ready to use or eat. One pound of pasta yields approximately 8 cups cooked pasta.

OVEN-FRIED POTATOES

Approximate cost: $.45
Protein grams: 12
Preparation time: 1 hour

Oven-frying creates no fewer calories than deep-frying, but these potatoes are much easier to prepare than deep-fried, and this is a popular dish with just about anyone (except those who are trying to diet).

3 **large potatoes**	**Salt and pepper**
Oil	

Scrub potatoes well and dry but do not peel them. Cut each potato in half lengthwise and then into finger-sized pieces about ½ inch in diameter. Spread out in shallow baking pan, and drip oil over top, turning pieces so that all sides are coated. Salt and pepper lightly, and put into 400-degree oven for 35 to 40 minutes, or until tender and browned. Turn occasionally with spatula while cooking. Serves 4 to 6.

●Hint: When planning to mash potatoes, rinse and drain them well after peeling, put them over the fire, and shake the pan until they are dry. This makes them creamier when they are mashed.●

❧HOLLANDAISE SAUCE❧

Here are two recipes for hollandaise sauce. The first contains the traditional ingredients, and it is made easily and quickly in the blender. The second version is made with yogurt, so it is lower in calories and more economical. The yogurt hollandaise sauce can be served hot or cold, and it reheats well.

BLENDER HOLLANDAISE SAUCE

Approximate cost: $1.60
Protein grams: 24
Preparation time: 12 to 15 minutes

8 egg yolks	1 cup (2 sticks)
1 teaspoon dry	melted butter
mustard	Salt
2 tablespoons lemon	Cayenne pepper
juice	

Blend egg yolks, mustard, and lemon juice, and add melted butter in a slow, steady stream. The mixture should thicken in the process. Add salt and cayenne pepper to taste. Keep warm over a pan of hot (but not boiling) water until ready to serve. Makes 1½ cups.

YOGURT HOLLANDAISE SAUCE

Approximate cost: $.60
Protein grams: 22
Preparation time: 12 minutes

Hot or cold, this is especially good over vegetables. And it works as nicely as a traditional hollandaise on poached eggs.

1 **cup unflavored yogurt**	**Dash cayenne pepper or hot**
2 **eggs, lightly beaten**	**pepper sauce**
½ **teaspoon salt**	

In the top of a double boiler over simmering water, put yogurt, eggs, and salt. Beat and stir gently with wire whisk until mixture thickens—about 10 minutes. When thickened, add a dash of cayenne pepper or hot pepper sauce. Makes 1¼ cups.

Note: If hollandaise sauce curdles, beat in 2 teaspoons of heavy cream or 1 well-beaten egg yolk to undo the damage.

GUACAMOLE

Approximate cost: $1.50
Protein grams: 14
Preparation time: 15 minutes

Guacamole is the wonderful avocado mixture from Mexico that has become a popular dip, spread, and topping for Mexican-American food. It should be eaten as soon as it is made.

3 **ripe avocados**	2 **tablespoons fresh, chopped cilantro**
⅓ **cup minced onion**	**(Chinese parsley)**
1 **clove garlic, mashed**	1 **tablespoon lime or lemon juice**
1 **tomato, peeled and diced (optional)**	**Pepper sauce**
	Salt

Peel avocados and remove seeds. Scoop out flesh, and mash until smooth. Add onion, garlic, tomato, cilantro, and lime or lemon juice, and mix well. Add hot pepper sauce and salt to taste. Makes about 2 cups.

OAT & COCONUT GRANOLA

Approximate cost: $3.75
Protein grams: 120
Preparation time: 45 minutes

½	cup sunflower seeds	5	cups rolled oats
½	cup sesame seeds	½	teaspoon salt
1	cup raw wheat germ	¾	cup honey
3	cups unsweetened, shredded coconut	½	cup safflower or corn oil
1	cup coarsely chopped almonds	2	teaspoons vanilla
		1	cup chopped dates or raisins

In a large bowl, combine seeds, wheat germ, coconut, almonds, and oats. Stir in salt. In a small saucepan, heat honey, oil, and vanilla, and pour over dry mixture, stirring to coat it well. Stir in dates or raisins. Spread in a shallow baking pan or pans ½-inch deep and bake in 350-degree oven for ½ hour, or until lightly browned. Stir frequently so edges do not brown too much. Cool and store in tightly covered containers in the refrigerator. Makes almost 3 quarts.

●Hint: If you are careful and pull off the skin of the avocado by hand, the flesh will not discolor unless you break the inner green surface. But if you do, rubbing it with lemon juice prevents discoloring.●

TABLES

WEIGHTS & MEASURES

THE METRIC SYSTEM

In the metric system, the *meter* is the fundamental unit of length, the *liter* is the fundamental unit of volume, and the *kilogram* is the fundamental unit of weight. The following prefixes, when combined with the basic unit names, provide the multiples and submultiples of the metric system.

milli . . . . one-thousandth (.001)
centi . . . . one-hundredth (.01)
deci . . . . one-tenth (.1)
deca . . . . ten (10)
hecto . . . . one hundred (100)
kilo . . . . one thousand (1,000)

☙☙☙

METRIC CONVERSION CHART

WEIGHT			
U.S. Units		Metric Equivalents	
Ounces (oz.)	Pounds (lb.)	Grams (g.)	Kilograms (kg.)
½	¹⁄₃₂	14.175	.014
1	¹⁄₁₆	28.35	.028
4	¼	113.40	.113
8	½	226.80	.227
12	¾	340.20	.340
16	1	453.60	.454

1 kilogram (1,000 grams) equals 2.2 pounds

TABLES

METRIC CONVERSION CHART
VOLUME

U.S. Units						Metric Equivalents	
Tea-spoons (tsp.)	Table-spoons (lbs.)	Fluid Ounces (fl. oz.)	Cups (c.)	Pints (pt.)	Quarts (qt.)	Deci-liters (dl.)	Liters (l.)
1	⅓	⅛	1/48			.05	.005
3	1	½	1/16			.15	.015
6	2	1	⅛	1/16		.30	.030
12	4	2	¼	⅛		.60	.060
24	8	4	½	¼	⅛	1.20	.120
36	12	6	¾	⅜	3/16	1.80	.180
48	16	8	1	½	¼	2.40	.240
				1	½	4.80	.480
				2	1	9.60	.960

Fractions of a cup in thirds are not shown in this table.

Note: Do not confuse the present British system with the metric system. British countries use the same system of weights we do, but their cooking utensils (cups and spoons) are slightly larger than those used in the United States and Canada. Great Britain is also now converting to the metric system.

TEMPERATURE CONVERSION CHART

Fahrenheit and Celsius (also known as centigrade) temperatures may be converted by using the following simple equation:

Fahrenheit = ⁹⁄₅ Celsius + 32 degrees
Celsius = ⁵⁄₉ Fahrenheit − 32 degrees

Fahrenheit	Celsius	Fahrenheit	Celsius	Fahrenheit	Celsius
−40	−40	149	65	329	165
−31	−35	150	65.5	338	170
−22	−30	158	70	347	175
−13	−25	167	75	350	176.6
− 4	−20	176	80	356	180
0	−17.7	185	85	365	185
5	−15	194	90	374	190
14	−10	200	93.3	383	195
23	− 5	203	95	392	200
*32	* 0	212	100	400	204.4
41	5	221	105	401	205
50	10	230	110	410	210
59	15	239	115	419	215
68	20	248	120	428	220
72	22.2	250	121.1	437	225
77	25	257	125	446	230
86	30	266	130	450	231.1
95	35	275	135	455	235
100	37.7	284	140	464	240
104	40	293	145	473	245
113	45	300	148.9	482	250
122	50	302	150	491	255
131	55	311	155	500	260
140	60	320	160	600	315.5

As you may have noticed, oven gauges (Fahrenheit scale) begin at 150 degrees (or warm) and increase by 25 degrees to 550 or 600 degrees (or broil). Celsius gauges will probably be numbered from 65 degrees to 315 degrees. *Water freezes at this temperature.

INDEX

INDEX

INDEX

Stew (*cont.*)
  lentil and eggplant, 6
  oyster, 70
Stuffing, bulgur-giblet, 47

Tabouli, 74
  see also Salad
Tacos, bean and rice, 9
Tamales, 31
Tofu dishes, 17–22
Tomato:
  rarebit, 10
  salad, 75
  sauce, 19, *see also* Sauce
Tortillas, 53
Tuna:
  and vegetable casserole, 66
  and vegetable chowder, 67
  canned, 59
  deviled, 65
  salad, 75, 76
Turbot, 60
Turkey:
  and herbed eggs, 57
  and rice meatballs, 56
  burgers, 55
  chowder, 58
  ground, 43, 54–6
  hash, 56
  lasagna, 55
  leftover, 56
  loaf, 54
  thighs, 58
  tostadas, 53

Vanilla cream and figs, 92
Vegetable(s):
  and lamb shanks, 35
  and tofu, 17
  casserole, 66
  curry, 16
  loaf with beef, 27
  salad, 72, 75
  sauce for, 105–6
  soup, 15, 67
  steamed, 74
  stir fried, 50

Weights and measures, 109–11

Zucchini:
  frittata, 12
  muffins, 90
  pizza, 12
  spaghetti, 63
  with squid, 65